Catherine Ponder

The Prospering
Power of Love

UNITY BOOKS

UNITY VILLAGE, MISSOURI

U NITY IS A link in the great educational movement inaugurated by Jesus Christ; our objective is to discern the truth in Christianity and prove it. The truth that we teach is not new, neither do we claim special revelations or discovery of new religious principles. Our purpose is to help and teach mankind to use and prove the eternal Truth taught by the Master.—*Charles Fillmore, founder of Unity*

CONTENTS

The Miracle of Love

SEVERAL years ago a businessman pointed out to me the success power of love. At the time, I was writing a series of prosperity articles for *Good Business*. Hearing of my project, this stockbroker asked, "What do you have in your series about love?" Startled, I replied: "About love? This series is on prosperity." "I know," he said. "But it won't be complete without an article on the prosperity law of love and good will. Love is the greatest success power there is."

Then he told me how he had developed his own private success formula for "straightening out" troublesome people. He stated that when

he became quiet and blessed them with an affirmation on love, it was as though an electric force
was generated, to which they became attuned.
Usually they responded quickly with harmonious
attitudes and behavior. If not, further affirmations on love invariably produced harmonious
results.

In recent times, we have heard much about
the success power of love. Dr. Smiley Blanton
has stated in his book "Love or Perish" that the
greatest human need is the need for love, and
that none of us can survive without it. Man
must have love in his life in some form or he
will perish. Love is the greatest power on earth,
he states.

There is nothing new about these ideas on
the power of love. It was the Master Psychol-
ogist of the ages who informed the lawyer that
love was the greatest of all the commandments.
Paul, one of the world's great intellectuals and
a builder of early Christianity, also ascribed all
power to love.

We are familiar with Henry Drummond's
famous essay on love, in which he writes about
Paul's epistle to the Corinthians. In his essay,
Drummond describes love as "the supreme gift,"
"the supreme good." He says, "The final test of
religion . . . is not religiousness, but love. . . .
You will find as you look back upon your life

that the moments that stand out, the moments when you have really lived, are the moments when you have done things in a spirit of love."

Drummond then describes the various aspects of love in Paul's epistle as patience, kindness, generosity, humility, courtesy, unselfishness, good temper, guilelessness, and sincerity. He tells of how a man read Paul's writings on love once a week for three months, and how this changed his whole life.

You and I might think of love in the terms Paul uses to describe it. We can express these qualities both as personal love and as impersonal love. Personal love could be expressed as kindness, tenderness, courtesy, affection, approval, consideration, appreciation, devotion to those in our family groups. Impersonal love is basically the ability to get along with people, without personal attachment or emotional involvement. *"I love all people and all people love me, without attachment"* is a fine statement to use often in developing a consciousness of impersonal love and good will toward our business associates and those in our workaday world.

I know of a group of persons who once experimented with the power of love in a prayer group and found it to be the greatest thing in the world to solve both personal and business problems. Once a week these persons met for an hour and affirmed statements of divine love. They brought to these meetings their private prayer lists of people and situations they wished to bless with the success power of love. No one else saw their prayer lists, nor did they talk about the people and problems their prayer lists represented.

Instead, they quietly placed their hands on their individual prayer lists while they affirmed together various statements on divine love. *"Divine love is doing its perfect work in me and through me now"* they affirmed for themselves, for their own health, wealth, and happiness; *"Divine love is doing its perfect work in you and through you now"* they affirmed for those on their prayer lists.

For a number of weeks they met and affirmed statements of love over and over. In a quiet way, amazing things began to happen to the various members of that group and to the people for whom they prayed. One businesswoman was out of harmony with a number of her friends. As she began dwelling on affirmations of love, her friends began appearing unexpectedly at the prayer group meetings, and reconciliation quickly took place.

Another businesswoman had been troubled for some time because of a misunderstanding that had arisen months previously between her and some friends. She had made every effort to apologize and bring about harmony and understanding again, but she had been coldly rebuffed in spite of her letters, telephone calls, and personal contacts.

One night during the regular prayer time as the group was affirming divine love for the names on the prayer lists, this woman and one other woman in the group both heard a popping noise in the air. The other woman discounted it, thinking it to be only her imagination. But after the meeting had concluded, the businesswoman came to her and confidentially said: "Did you hear that popping sound in the air? That wasn't your imagination; it really happened! That was the hard thoughts that have existed between me and my friends. I'm convinced that tonight, through our spoken words, divine love dissolved the hard thoughts and the inharmony that has existed between us. That was the dissolving power of love that you heard healing that situation!"

From that night on she had a completely different feeling about the situation. She felt peaceful and harmonious. She quietly gave thanks that divine understanding had been established and that divine love had healed the previous misunderstanding and hostility.

Some weeks later, though no outer change

had come, she felt led to contact her friends
again. This time, instead of rebuffing her, they
reacted as though nothing had ever been wrong
between them. The previous cordiality, understanding, and friendship were reestablished and
continue even now.

Perhaps you do not have access to such a
prayer group. But you can still experience the
success power of love. You have all the love
you need for healing, prosperity, and happy
human relationships right *within* yourself. Divine love is one of your mental and spiritual
faculties. You do not have to search outside
yourself for love. You can begin releasing it
from within outward, through your thoughts,
words, actions, and affirmative prayers. As you
do, you will experience the success power of
love in all its fullness as it works through people, situations, and conditions that concern you.

A world-renowned sociologist, Sorokin, has
conducted research studies at Harvard University on the power of love. Under his direction, a
staff of scientists studied the subject of love.
Their findings were that love, like other good
things, can be produced deliberately by human
beings. They stated that there is no reason why
we cannot learn to generate love as we do other
natural forces.

Thus there is no reason for you to feel disillusioned or disappointed if love has seemingly let you down or passed you by. Those who bitterly declare that their lives are without love are mistakenly looking to someone or something outside themselves for love. Begin realizing now that love is first *within* you and can be released through your thoughts, feelings, words, and actions. As you begin developing love from within outward, you are truly proving your method to be spiritual, scientific, and satisfying. You no longer feel at the mercy of people, situations, and conditions. You become master of your world and free from hurt, fear, disappointment, and disillusionment.

As the stockbroker said, it is like developing an electric force. Love will begin to radiate outwardly into every part of your world, to attract to you the right people, situations, and conditions that will add to your success and happiness. You will soon realize that instead of your being at the mercy of the world, the world responds to your own thoughts and feelings; and that when your thoughts and feelings generate love, the world about you will happily respond in a most wonderful way! This is the success power of love.

Many people are discovering this power in all departments of life. In the realm of human relationships it is all-powerful. A housewife told of having quarreled with her husband, after which he stormed out of the house. Having learned that she could generate love from within outward, she decided to try it in this marital crisis. Quietly she began to say over and over: *"I call on divine love to heal our marriage now. I call on divine love to straighten out and adjust this situation."*

In a little while a sense of peace overwhelmed her, and she busily began preparing dinner for her husband in the faith that he would return to enjoy it. (After previous quarrels, it had not always been so.) Soon she heard the door open, and her husband entered, in a happy frame of mind, carrying a box of candy for her. Their quarrels became fewer and less severe, and in due time their marriage was entirely healed of inharmony.

A businesswoman related a similar experience concerning the power of love in her marriage, which had been unhappy for some time. There had been many quarrels—much bickering, tension, inharmony. One night when there had been a prolonged and bitter quarrel, the woman thought: "We cannot go on. This inharmony is affecting our health, our business success, and our marriage. There must be a way out."

She began looking for something to read that might give her a sense of peace and hope, and she found these words: *"Love melts situations that seem impossible."* Over and over she said: "Yes, it is true. *Love melts situations that seem impossible."*

Formerly, reconciliation had come slowly and painstakingly after each quarrel. But as she continued dwelling on this statement of love, the inharmony and misunderstanding faded almost at once. That proved to be this couple's last bitter quarrel. Since that time whenever inharmony has seemed near, she has quickly affirmed, *"Love melts situations that seem impossible";* always this has cleared the air and harmony has been reestablished.

Do you doubt that your thoughts and words of divine love can have equal power in your own life and affairs? Several years ago, I had a simple family experience that convinced me that our thoughts of love do reach others more quickly and completely than we sometimes realize. One warm spring day I was in my study, trying to finish an article on love, when my teen-age son came in. He had been playing golf all day, and was hungry and anxious to get home.

When I explained that I was trying to complete an article and would finish in a few minutes, he quietly left my study. Soon I thought I heard the study door open again, but since things at once became quiet again, I did not turn from my work to investigate. Some minutes later, when I had completed my work, I realized that my son had quietly returned and placed two red roses on my desk from the nearby rose garden. Without a word he had then left, to wait patiently for me. He had not known I was working on an article on love. Never before had he brought me flowers, but at that moment he seemed attuned to the very ideas I was dwelling on in the article, and he lovingly responded.

On still another occasion, he demonstrated to me the success power of love. One morning he left for school in an unhappy mood. All day I remembered it and felt badly that he had begun the day in such a state of mind. I felt that there was something I should have done or said to turn the tide of his thinking in the morning. All day as I remembered this incident I kept affirming, *"Divine love is doing its perfect work in this situation now."*

That afternoon when he arrived home from school, he came into the house, put aside his books, and greeted me with the words, "Hi, beautiful!" I cannot remember when he had greeted me in such a manner before, but truly, love *had* done its perfect work that day.

When you are inclined to wonder how thoughts and words of love can do much good in resolving various problems, remind yourself that loving words and loving thoughts seem supercharged with power to produce good. Indeed, it is the mission of love, both personally and impersonally, to produce eternal good in your life. Your part is not to wonder how love works, but just to dare to begin releasing it, from *within* yourself. When you do, you will always witness interesting and satisfying results.

Several years ago a doctor showed me a medical book on psychosomatic illness. In this book a group of doctors had compiled their analyses of various illnesses, and of the mental and emotional attitudes they felt caused these illnesses. I was amazed to see that in every analysis the need for love was listed.

For instance, in the case of stomach disorders of all types, one of the psychosomatic reasons given for such illness was "love needed." In the case of heart disorders, one of the reasons listed was "love needed."

In the case of skin disorders, one of the reasons listed was "need for approval," which is a form of love. (A bookkeeper stated that while experiencing a skin disorder she began a daily practice of placing her hands on her face and affirming, *"Divine love is healing you now,"* and the skin disorder soon faded.)

In the case of female disorders, one of the reasons listed was "need for love." In the case of chronic fatigue, one of the psychosomatic reasons listed was "depression, insecurity, and need for love."

In the case of the common headache and migraine, one of the reasons listed was "insecurity and need for love." In the case of excessive weight and overeating, one of the reasons listed was "a feeling of dissatisfaction with life and a need for love." In the case of alcoholism and other excesses, one of the reasons listed was "feelings of inferiority and need for love."

The wonderful thing to remember is that when there is a need for love, we can begin supplying it from *within* ourselves. A businessman told me that he was healed of a painful condition of long standing after he began releasing love from within himself, by speaking words of love to his body. He had tried various treatments to no avail, and then he heard of the healing power of love. He began placing his hand on the painful area of his body, saying over and over, *"I love you."* The pain subsided, and gradually faded away.

Cancer has been described as an "anxiety disease." The emotional histories of a large percentage of those who have cancer show that in some period of their lives they felt anxious, insecure, or unloved, and that they subconsciously retained that feeling, which had often turned to bitterness, a critical state of mind, and may have even generated hostility and hate.

One authority has stated that sixty-two per cent of his cancer patients told stories of loss, intense grief, depression, and despair that led up to their physical condition. As long ago as 1925, an analyst declared that after studying hundreds of cancer patients, she found most of them had suffered some important emotional crisis prior to the development of the disease, and that they had been unable to find effective outlets for their deep feelings and emotions.

In the field of prosperity, love as impersonal good will is all-powerful too. It has been estimated that only fifteen percent of a person's financial success is due to his technical ability, while eighty-five percent is due to his ability to get along with people. Personnel managers agree that more than two thirds of the people who lose their jobs do so not because of incompetence, but because they cannot get along with others. Approximately ten percent are discharged because of inadequate preparation for the skills needed, whereas the other ninety percent are fired because of "personality problems."

A secretary once realized that in order to keep her job, which was interesting and wellpaying, she would have to learn how to cope

with her employer's unpleasant "morning disposition." She learned of the success power of
love and began using one of Emmet Fox's statements: *"All men are expressions of divine love;
therefore, I can meet with nothing but the expressions of divine love."*

Beginning her day with this statement helped
to establish a peaceful atmosphere in the office
for her employer's arrival. By the time he called
her in for dictation, divine love had done its
perfect work on his disposition. In time, his
morning grouchiness and moodiness were re-
placed with a consistent pleasant disposition.
The secretary felt her work in this regard was
highly worth while, since her boss' disposition
had been the only unfavorable and worrisome
aspect of her job.

Financially, an attitude of love is worth
while, too. A traveling salesman who was heavily in debt attempted to get a loan from a bank
to pay off his debts. Because he lacked collateral,
he was not able to get the loan. He began to
affirm, *"God prospers me now."* Within a few
days he made a large sale and was able to pay
off all his debts, with ample money left over.

A number of years ago during a financial
recession, and in bitter cold weather, the firm
for which I was working experienced financial
difficulties. Members of the board of directors

had become depressed because of the weather, which seemed to be delaying the firm's prosperity. They were also depressed about general economic conditions. It seemed a hopeless situation until several persons working for the firm agreed to begin affirming together, at specific times, statements on the prospering power of love. Each individual affirmed for himself and his own inspiration: *"I am the love of God in expression. I let God's love guide, direct, and inspire me."* The statement used for the firm's prosperity was: *"God's love in us is drawing to us new ideas, new courage, and visible daily supply. God's love in you is drawing to you new ideas, new courage, and visible daily supply."*

The atmosphere of depression and hopelessness concerning the business situation seemed to lift. Continued use of the prayers caused all those involved to experience an uplifted state of mind. New ideas and new courage attracted visible daily supply. Within a few weeks the financial crisis had passed, and that year proved to be one of the most prosperous the firm has ever known!

A chiropractor who was having similar financial challenges asked how this firm managed to make a financial comeback in the midst of bad weather and economic recession. The prayers were shared with him, and his financial results were so satisfying that he obtained a thousand printed copies of the prayers, which he distributed to his patients whenever they mentioned their own financial challenges. Thus the power of love proved its prospering power to many people that winter in our area alone.

Many years ago, Emma Curtis Hopkins gave some financial advice along this line when she wrote, "Take your business as it is, and praise divine love that there is a strong, wise way out of your dilemma." When there is such a need, affirm, *"I praise divine love that there is a strong, wise way out of this dilemma."*

In all phases of life, love is a success power. Many persons who are seeking a balanced life have found this prayer helpful: *"Divine love, expressing through me, now draws to me all that is needed to make me happy and my life complete."*

Whatever your need in life may be, love is the answer. You do not have to look outside yourself for love. Begin releasing it from within your own thoughts and feelings, and you will attract to you whatever people, situations, and conditions are for your highest good. Truly, *"You walk in the charmed circle of God's love, and you are divinely irresistible to your highest good now."* This is the prospering power of love.

Love Your Way to Success

Hᴏᴡ ᴏꜰᴛᴇɴ we try to battle our way through life, experiencing disappointment, pain, and failure at every turn, when we could much more easily love our way through life, experiencing success every step of the way!

Emmet Fox once wrote, "There is no difficulty that enough love will not conquer."

I recall once having a problem that (I thought) I had tried in every way to solve. Still it was as though I faced a stone wall.

Other persons were involved. Until they took action, I was helpless to do anything more, I reasoned. It seemed a particularly frustrating

situation since the next move had to be made by
someone else. I had prodded these persons in
every way I knew and still they had not taken
action. It seemed hopeless, until one day I read
these words by Emma Curtis Hopkins:

"Everything is really full of love for you
. . . The good that is for you loves you as much
as you love it. The good that is for you seeks you
and will come flying to you if you see that what
you love is love itself. All people will change
when you know that they are love. We shall
change toward all people when we know that
we ourselves are formed out of love. All is love.
There is nothing in all the universe but love."

When I read those words, it was as though
something hard broke up inside of me. I actually
felt something hard move in the area of the
heart; then it seemed to dissolve and I was able
to breathe more freely.

Truly, there had been a stone wall in this
situation, just as I had sensed. But that stone
wall had not been an outer physical structure
towering over me. The stone wall was actually
within me, in the form of my own hard thoughts
about the situation. It was a revelation, a sur-
prise, and finally a relief to realize that not
someone else, but my own hard thinking had
been the barrier that had caused the situation to
remain at a standstill.

I began to affirm: *"Everything is really full of love for me, including those persons. The good that is for me in this situation loves me, as much as I love it. The good that is for me in this matter now seeks me, and comes flying to me as I behold this situation with love."*

Within a few days I heard from the persons involved, though I had not heard from them previously for many months. Their letter seemed especially cordial, and it stated that they were immediately expediting the matter in which I was interested. Now, whenever I have any business contact with this firm, they always respond graciously and speedily. Never since that time has there been any delay or misunderstanding.

You can love your way through any troublesome situation by declaring: *"This person and this situation are really full of love for me, and I am full of love for them. I praise divine love in this matter now. I behold this situation with love."*

Some years ago I had another experience that proved to me that there is nothing weak about love; that love can win more battles than fists or weapons; that love is our "secret weapon" for successful results.

I was asked to take a job as director of a nonprofit organization. It was a job that no one else wanted because there had been great inharmony in this organization. Along with the ill feeling that had been generated, financial lack had also appeared. It was not a job to look forward to, especially since this would be my first assignment after entering a new field of work. I had proper training for the job, but no experience. This hardly seemed a proper assignment for an inexperienced person, but it was this job or none for the present, so I reluctantly took it.

At the first meeting with the board of directors of the organization, things did not look promising. Two of the directors objected to my job appointment, saying that I was too young and inexperienced to straighten things out. Silently, I agreed with them wholeheartedly. But the other board members pointed out that I was the new director, having been trained and assigned to this job by the home office; that they planned to work with me to straighten out difficulties in whatever way I felt best.

In praying for guidance about this challenging job, the thought came to me that divine love was to be my secret weapon; that love could win in this situation and could again bring victorious results of harmony and prosperity to this organization.

When I expressed these thoughts at that first board meeting, my ideas on divine love only provoked the two objecting board members, who scoffed at the "mere" power of love for solving anything. They "told me off" for even suggesting such a thing, and then they resigned. This proved to be love's first step in clearing away inharmony.

In private conversation, the chairman of the board of directors agreed with me that there was nothing weak about divine love; that divine love could win this battle. He believed so strongly in the harmonizing, prospering power of love to make things right that he agreed to meet with me for an hour every morning so that we might discuss the various affairs of the organization and affirm the perfect results of divine love.

The affirmations we used in those daily morning meetings were: *"Divine love is doing its perfect work here and now. Divine love harmonizes, divine love adjusts, divine love prospers. Divine love foresees everything and richly provides every good thing for this organization now. Divine love is now victorious!"*

The results of those daily meetings were almost unbelievable. As we poured forth words of divine love into this troubled situation, it was like pouring out a healing balm. Attitudes and actions became quiet, peaceful, harmonious, cooperative. Soon it seemed as though there had never been any difficulty in the organization.

Peace and harmony reigned in all its activities.

As we continued daily affirmations of divine love, new people, new activity, new prosperity flowed into this organization. The financial income soon doubled. A number of gifts came, including fresh paint and willing painters who applied it free of charge to the building. New drapes, lovely new furnishings, air conditioners, a public-address system, and other needed equipment were provided. The entire building that housed the organization was beautifully redecorated within a few months.

The organization went on to new growth, new progress, new prosperity. Soon no one spoke of or cared about the former trouble; everything was so wonderful in the present. Though I am no longer connected with that organization, it has continued to grow and prosper over the years. Divine love met and solved my challenges there; divine love has continued to do its perfect work in that group.

A housewife decided to use love as her secret weapon in a troublesome situation. For months she had been speaking of her "no-good" husband. He was a miner who left home every spring to find work in the gold and silver mines of the Northwest. Usually after he left for the mines, she did not hear from him again until late fall, when he came home to loaf all winter.

During the summer months, she was left at home alone to work as a waitress, or to do anything else she could to feed and clothe herself and pay the bills. She had been contemplating divorce because life with her husband seemed a hopeless struggle for existence.

It was then that she learned of the problem-solving power of love. Instead of continuing to dwell upon her husband's faults, she began to decree that divine love was doing its perfect work in her marriage, in their financial affairs, and in her husband's job prospects. Good things began to happen.

Her husband wrote her that he had obtained work in a silver mine and that he would begin sending money home regularly when he received his first pay check. Since he had never previously sent money home, this seemed a miracle. Though in the past he had not written at all when he was away, he now wrote long, friendly letters regularly, even speaking of his desire for them to have a good life together.

At the end of the summer mining season he wrote that he had obtained work for the winter, too. This was unusual since his type of work had always been seasonal. As his wife continued to affirm the perfect outworking of divine love, their marriage became completely harmonized, their debts of long standing were paid, and her

husband recently formed his own mining corporation and is now in business for himself. He
is now helping her start her own business which
she will conduct when he is away in the mines.
It is a business that they will work in together
when he is not otherwise occupied.

How often people have missed the blessings
and security of a happy marriage and a good
life because they have condemned and criticized,
rather than loved their way through the challenges that confronted them! Yet how much
easier it is to love your way through a problem
than to battle your way through it!

The unloving, unnecessary results that people often bring on themselves through criticism
(the opposite of love) recall the story of the
young artist who had a genius (he thought) for
picking out the faults and weaknesses of other
people. He prided himself on seeing the unworthy traits in their character. One night this
young man had a dream in which he saw himself
walking on a barren road, struggling wearily
beneath a heavy burden.

In the dream he cried out weakly: "What is
this heavy weight I have to carry? Why must I
carry it? Why should I be so burdened?" A
voice answered: "Your burden is the weight of
all the faults you have found in other people.
Why do you complain? You discovered those

faults. Should they not, therefore, belong to you?"

The description of evil doubles the appearance of evil. Whatever of evil you see in others, you are inviting into your own life in some form of negation. When you "run down" someone else with your criticism and condemnation, you are opening the way for your own mind, body, or affairs to become "run down" with ill health, unhappiness, confusion, or financial lack.

A group of employees withdrew from a business firm because they did not like the new manager. Then they continued to belittle and condemn the new manager after they were no longer connected with the firm. As they continued in their negative judgments, one of these former employees had a heart attack and died within a few months. Another former employee opened a new business; it soon failed. Later he opened several other businesses, and they failed. He also became estranged from several members of his family.

Other former employees of the firm who remained critical had similar destructive experiences to meet. One businesswoman had a stroke, developed paralysis, and passed on within a year, though she previously had enjoyed many healthy years of active living. Another person developed arthritis, and soon could walk only on crutches. Still another person had several bouts of pneumonia and had to be hospitalized frequently. Physical suffering was also attended by heavy financial expense, and by other business problems. The unjust criticisms these people had meant for someone else hurt only themselves.

As for the new manager, he was aware of the backstairs gossip but he ignored it, for he knew it had no power; and both he and his business prospered.

The ancients knew another success secret we should know: The description of good doubles good! May Rowland in her book *Dare to Believe!* has described how you can double the good in your life:

"If you are not attracting the good that you desire in your life, learn to express love; become a radiating center of love; and you will find that love, the divine magnet within you, will change your whole world. . . . When your heart is filled with love you will not be critical or irritable, but you will be divinely irresistible."

Florence Scovel Shinn wrote, "Every man on this planet is taking his initiation in love." Whatever your problem, it is but a test in love. If you meet that test through love, your problem will be solved. If you do not meet that test through love, your problem will assail until you do! Your problem is your initiation in love.

A businesswoman recently related how she met her initiation in love:

"Only a short time ago, I felt I could not go on. My husband was on the brink of a nervous breakdown and in deep depression. Our oldest son, age nineteen, was struggling to stay in college, doing it all on his own, without a dime of help from us. Our middle son, age twelve, had been under treatment for several years as an emotionally disturbed child. He has periods of becoming quite angry, on the edge of violence. Our daughter, age eleven, was beginning to react to all this discord with temper tantrums and sulking spells, and seemed unable to get along harmoniously with her friends or teachers. I kept getting one kidney infection after another. Since I have only one kidney, you can understand the concern I felt when my doctor warned me to be especially careful.

"After reading an article about the power of divine love to improve personalities, situations, events, even one's health, I bought a notebook and a pen. Every time I started to worry, feel sick or afraid, I sat down, relaxed, wrote the name of the family member or the situation that was bothering me, and then I wrote down a decree of love about it. For my husband, our children, and for myself, I often wrote over and

over: *'I behold you with the eyes of love and I
glory in your perfection.'*

"The results were almost unbelievable! My
husband was at a standstill when I began using
the power of love on our affairs six weeks ago.
Recently he took a bath, the first in weeks; he
got his hair cut and turned out some work on his
own, without a word of prodding from me. Our
son in college received a one-hundred-dollar
refund on income tax. He also got a job manag-
ing the baseball team, so his tuition will be provided. Our middle son has gone for several
weeks now without displaying violent behavior.
His disposition has greatly improved. Our
daughter is getting along better with her friends
and teachers. As for my kidney infection, it has
cleared up completely, and I am now launching
on a health program to build up my resistance.
I have also obtained a part-time job. You can
see why I shall always be grateful that I learned
about the problem-solving power of love!"

Charles Fillmore has written, "The more we
talk about love, the stronger it grows in the consciousness, and if we persist in thinking loving
thoughts and speaking loving words, we are sure
to bring into our experience the feeling of that
great love that is beyond description—the very
love of God. . . .

"You may trust love to get you out of your

difficulties. There is nothing too hard for it to accomplish for you, if you put your confidence in it."

Love works in varied ways to produce right results, when it is recognized and called forth in a situation. As you begin to think more about how you can love your way through life, rather than about how you have to battle your way through life, love will reveal to you its secret success powers. Launch forth on the great venture of love, and affirm often along the way: *"I live by the law of love, and love is now victorious."* This one thought can win many a battle in your life.

Love Works
a Healing Power

PART OF THE spring season is the religious observance of Lent, usually considered a period of prayer and fasting, which symbolizes a time of preparation for the resurrection of new life and beauty in one's personal world.

Let us stop crucifying and start resurrecting during the Lenten season! We can do it through the healing power of love.

What you should do is fast from negative memories of the past—grudges, criticisms, spite, feelings of injustice and hurt, as well as other inharmonies. There are definite, simple ways you can pour out the healing power of love on your negative memories, so that you can be free of them forever. As you do become free of these destructive emotions, you cease crucifying yourself and others and you are then ready for resurrected good.

There are two special ways you can fast from negative attitudes, and tune in on the healing power of love, which makes you whole in mind, body, and affairs. These special ways are the act of release, and the act of forgiveness. Perhaps it surprises you to hear that release and forgiveness are part of love. Yet when you find that other phases of love have not healed some troublesome condition in your life, you may discover that it is because you have not invoked the releasing, forgiving phases of love. When you do, satisfying results will surely come.

Kahlil Gibran might have been describing these two important phases of love when he wrote: "Speak to us of love. . . . Even as he [love] is for your growth so is he for your pruning . . . think not you can direct the course of love, for love, if it finds you worthy, directs your course." You have heard it said that love is a many-splendored thing, but often when the pruning power of love is at work in your life you may have felt that love is a "many-splintered" thing. When you are willing to release and forgive, the splinter (or "thorn in the flesh") is transformed into a splendid result, and you find that love is able to direct your course to greater good.

Through release and forgiveness you break up, cross out, dissolve, and are freed forever from the negative attitudes and memories that have limited you to less than the highest and best in your life experience.

The freeing, forgiving attitude likewise "raises" your good and brings it to life. Invoke the healing power of love through freeing and forgiving the negative experiences of your past and present, and you will find yourself well on the way to resurrected good during this Lenten season.

It is the law that you must forgive if you want to demonstrate over your own difficulties and make any real spiritual progress. Many people consider *forgive* an unpleasant word, but it means simply to set free, to liberate, by "giving" something positive in place of or "for" something negative.

Release is a form of forgiveness that we all need to practice often. Although we usually think of emotional attachment as one of the highest forms of love, quite the opposite is true. Emotional *release* is one of the highest forms of love. Attachment leads to bondage, whereas the way of true love is to free that which you love.

You never lose anything through release. Instead, you open the way for a freer, more satisfying type of love to develop, where everyone involved is able to give and receive love in a more harmonious way.

You never lose that which is for your highest good, under any circumstances. When it seems that you have lost something, it is because it is no longer best for you. Though you may feel that it is still best, you have actually outgrown it, and the pruning power of love has released you from it. Realizing this, you are able to free it and open your mind and heart to receive your new and higher good.

Setting others free means setting yourself free. When you feel bound to other people, their attitudes, their behavior, their way of life, it is because you are (perhaps unconsciously) binding them to you. Then you begin to feel bound, chafing against the very bondage you have caused! Always you yourself hold the key to your freedom from bondage. You turn the key to that freedom when you release the personality, problem, or condition that you think is clutching you. Remember you are the master, never the slave, of circumstances.

You become victor instead of victim when you dare to speak the word of release to the person or thing you think is binding you. You are your own bondage made manifest. You can become your own release made manifest, too.

A housewife had worried for many months over her husband's illness. The more she tried to help him recover, the more he seemed to cling to his illness and the more confined they both were. One day she learned of the healing power of release and began to declare for her husband: *"I release you now to your highest good. I love you and I release you to complete freedom and complete health in whatever way is best. I am free and you are free."*

When this woman had previously tried to help her husband by using various healing affirmations, he had seemed subconsciously to resist her attempts to will him to health. After she began to release him to find health in his own way, ceasing any mental effort in his direction, and began to lead a more normal life herself, her husband's health rapidly improved. Some of his former ailments disappeared completely. He experienced the healing power of love as it worked through release.

Most human-relations problems would melt away if people would practice the healing power of release, instead of trying to make people over in a certain image, or trying to force them to do things in a certain way.

Nowhere is there more need for the expression of love as release than between husbands and wives, between parents and children. We often try to bend others to our will, calling it love when it is really selfish possessiveness that binds instead of frees. Then we wonder why others resist instead of accepting our "help."

Gibran described the loving attitude of release in marriage: "Love one another, but make not a bond of love . . . let there be spaces in your togetherness. . . . Sing and dance together and be joyous, but let each one of you be alone . . . stand together yet not too near together."

He described the loving attitude of release toward children in these words: "Your children are not your children. They are the sons and daughters of Life's longing for itself. They come through you but not from you, and though they are with you yet they belong not to you. . . . You may house their bodies but not their souls. . . . You may strive to be like them, but seek not to make them like you."

A counselor was once called to a hospital to visit a young woman who had experienced a nervous breakdown. She was having severe headaches and prolonged crying spells. Drugs and medication had brought no relief.

Her mother was frantic with fear, saying: "I can't understand what has happened. This girl has always been such an obedient child. She has never disagreed with me, nor crossed me in any way. But now she is saying terrible things to me. She tells me I've ruined her life, that I have kept her from getting a job and working; that I've kept her from marrying and having a normal life. To be sure, I never encouraged her to work, because she had always been a timid, sickly child. There was no financial reason for her to work, and so I insisted that she remain at home and help out there, thinking it would provide her with a more pleasant way of life. Now she is criticizing and condemning me for it. She suddenly seems to hate me."

Her daughter, who was finally rebelling against her mother's domination and "smother love," was hardly a child. She was past thirty, though she still wore bobby socks, long hair, and teen-age clothes. She also seemed to think and talk like a teenager.

The daughter felt quite guilty about having turned against her mother, but she said she could not help it. When assured by the counselor that she was reacting in a normal way, she began to relax. As she did, the severe headaches left her completely. Her crying ceased. She was able to retain food again, and soon her strength returned. Much of the hostility toward her mother soon faded away.

Further talks with this mother and daughter helped them both to realize that this experience had been for good. Had this daughter not been able to release her accumulated hostilities toward her mother, had she not been able to begin claiming her emotional independence, she would doubtless have faced confinement in a mental hospital. The statistics of mental illness show that most of it arises from inharmonious relationships in the home—relationships that are usually possessive and dominating. Mental illness is the patient's way of fighting that domination and escaping from possessiveness.

Your dear ones must have liberty to live their own lives, and you must grant it to them, or else you will create problems for them and for yourself. If you want to free yourself from all types of problems in mind, body, and affairs, you must release others to find their good in their own way. A clear channel is then opened for great good to come to all involved. Your own freedom and well-being depend upon such release, as do the freedom and well-being of your loved ones.

A professional woman was quite concerned about her bachelor son. He was very successful in his work but had never married, and still lived with his mother. A widow, she devoted many years of her life to rearing and educating this son. Now the time had come when she wished to be free to travel and perhaps to work elsewhere. She also longed to see her son happily married. She realized that her own freedom and well-being depended upon such emotional release of her son.

Then it seemed that her dreams were coming true: her son met the girl of his choice. But instead of being happy about it, his mother became upset and resentful, constantly finding fault with the girl. Soon she became ill, and her physician told her that she was suffering from hypertension caused by some secret anxiety.

She then realized that in order to be free from illness, in order to live a happy, balanced life, she must free her son to live his life as he wished. She realized that setting him free meant setting herself free. For this purpose she constantly affirmed: *"I fully and freely release you. I loose you and let you go to your good. The good of one is the good of all."* Before long all anxiety left her, her health improved, and her son was married. This left her free to travel, to seek new work, and to develop a whole new, freer way of life that she had long wanted.

When your prayers have not been answered, it is often because you need to practice release —release of some person or situation, some financial or health problem. Often it is not an enemy you need to release but a friend, a relative—a husband, wife, or child. As you practice release, your problem is solved, your good is resurrected.

Forgiveness is a very important type of release, and a most important form of love. When you practice forgiveness, you experience the healing power of love. You must forgive injuries and hurts of the past and present—not so much for the other person's sake as for your own. Resentment, condemnation, anger, the desire to "get even" or to see someone punished or hurt, are things that rot your soul. Such attitudes fasten your troubles to you. They bind you to many other problems which actually have nothing whatever to do with the original grievances.

Emmet Fox has explained: "When you hold resentment against anyone, you are bound to that person by a cosmic link, a real though mental chain. You are tied by a cosmic tie to the thing that you hate. The one person perhaps in the whole world whom you most dislike is the very one to whom you are attaching yourself by a hook that is stronger than steel."

A housewife recently described how the healing power of love worked in her family through forgiveness: "Ten months ago my whole world seemed to have crashed to pieces. My husband's job, managerial in nature, was

suddenly (and apparently unfairly) terminated.
Two of our children and I were very sick with
bronchial infections. I also had a recurrence of a
bladder infection. It was at this hopeless point
in our affairs that I was introduced to your book
How to Live a Prosperous Life, which I began
to study. In the first chapter I learned something
I needed very much: *'I fully and freely forgive.
I loose and let go. I cast all judgments, resent-
ments, criticism, and unforgiveness upon the
Christ within, to be dissolved and healed. The
prospering Truth has set me free to meet my
rich good and to share my good with others.'*

"As I read these words, I realized I had been
openly resentful toward my husband's former
employer because of his seeming unfairness and
poor business judgment. I kept using the affirmations in the book and actually it became very
easy to forgive completely.

"Within the next few days my infection was
gone, a skin ailment of my mother's disappeared,
and then our financial demonstrations began!
Our debts had seemed insurmountable; but
gradually, through a complete change of mind
brought about by forgiveness, money began to
come from unexpected sources. We received an
income-tax refund; my parents sent money to
cover the rent; our creditors did not press us for
money. After being unemployed for two months,

my husband was led to the right job, one which he thoroughly understands, as general manager of a ski resort which is under construction now and which we will move to shortly. The corporation is building us a wonderful apartment, fully carpeted and decorated to our taste."

When we hold resentment toward another, we are bound to that person or condition by a cosmic link, and forgiveness is the only way to dissolve that link and be free.

In the pamphlet *The Way through Gethsemane,* Cleda Reyner points out that since other persons are children of God, there is really nothing to forgive. They have not really failed us, or disappointed us, or let us down, or shamed us. They may have stumbled while crossing our pathway. But they were sons of God who had temporarily lost their way. If they crossed our pathway, it was because they needed and wanted our blessing. They were unconsciously looking to us to be steadied and set right.

Our progress has not been hindered, no matter what they did or did not do. They did not, they could not, keep our good from us. They crossed our path by divine appointment, even though they seemed to hurt us for a little while. When people bother us in any way, it is because their souls are trying to get our divine attention, and our blessing. When we give them that, they no longer bother us. They fade out of our lives and find their good elsewhere.

A nurse found great comfort and truth in these words, after she was seriously injured in a collision with a car driven by an intoxicated man. After recovering she returned to her nursing profession. Again and again the man responsible for the collision was admitted to the hospital where she worked—and always he was in an intoxicated state. She refused to nurse him, and was assured by his doctor that she would not be assigned to his case.

Once when he was admitted, there was a shortage of nurses on her floor, and she was the only nurse available when the light came on in his room. Since it was unavoidable, she took him his tray and medicine. When she appeared, he recognized her, talked about the accident, and told her he had been worried about her financial affairs after the accident, realizing that she was widowed with children to care for.

In the wee hours of the morning, as they talked, he asked her forgiveness, and she gave it. The amazing thing was that, following their conversation, he gradually stopped drinking, and she never heard of his being admitted to the hospital again. She realized that the man seemed to have wanted her forgiveness and blessing. When he got that, he faded out of her life.

If you do not know what or who it is you need to forgive, when your good seems withheld from you, ask God to reveal to you what or whom you need to forgive. You may be surprised to find where the block is!

A woman discovered a lump in her breast and was greatly frightened by it. But instead of rushing out to talk about it to anyone, she decided to analyze the situation mentally and pray for guidance.

She realized that a hard condition in the body symbolizes a hard condition in the mind —hard thoughts of resentment, condemnation, unforgiveness. She prayed, "Divine Intelligence, what or whom do I need to forgive?"

Since the answer did not come immediately, she continued every day to pray, meditate, and ask: "Divine Intelligence, what or whom do I need to forgive? What hard attitudes do I need to release, give up, in order to be forgiven this condition?" In meditation one day she found herself thinking about her husband and a woman with whom he had been involved five years previously. At the time, she had met the experience nonresistantly, and it had faded away. She and her husband were now happier than ever, but she realized in this meditation period that she still had hard thoughts toward the other woman and toward her husband concerning the distressing experiences during that period.

She prayed for the other woman, blessed her, released her, saying to her mentally: *"I freely forgive you. I let you go. You have gone to meet your good and to share your good elsewhere. It is done, it is finished."* To her husband she mentally said: *"I freely forgive you. I let go all false concepts about you. You are a faithful, loving husband, and we have a wonderful marriage. Only good has come from that experience."*

She declared these words of forgiveness in her prayer time for several weeks. One day she realized that the lump in her breast was gone; she never knew when it disappeared.

Make this Lenten season a rewarding season by deliberately practicing the healing power of love through acts of forgiveness and release. Charles Fillmore describes this as a "sure remedy" for resurrecting health, wealth, and happiness: "Bless your problem, whatever it be, with a thought somewhat like this: *I now release you and bless you. Divine love is adjusting my life and its problems. Realizing this, I abide in peace. . . .* Every person who thus allies himself with the power of divine love creates a bit of heaven on earth."

The Resurrecting Power of Love

THE WORD *resurrect* means "to bring to view again . . . to restore to life." The resurrection of Jesus Christ was for the purpose of bringing to view again the divine nature of all mankind.

Man was created with a divine nature, in the image of God. But man misused his divine nature by turning his attention to a belief in evil, and so man forgot about his divinity or how to use it.

Some of the great characters of the Old Testament tried to bring back to notice, to use, the divine nature of man. David sang of man's divinity:

"Yet thou hast made him little less than
    God,
 and dost crown him with glory and honor."
"You are gods,
 Sons of the Most High, all of you."

Job realized, "It is the spirit in a man."

Spiritual man has always been crowned with
glory and honor, though mankind lost sight of
its glorious divinity for many centuries. In order
to bring to view again, to restore to life, man's
divinity, a loving Father sent a Savior, a Re-
deemer—One who would resurrect the divinity
of all mankind.

The raising up of the Christ nature in the
man Jesus symbolizes the resurrection of the
Christ nature in all mankind. Jesus described
man's divinity when He said, "The kingdom of
God is in the midst of you." What theology calls
a "lost soul" is merely a soul that has lost sight
of its divinity. When our divine nature is
brought back into view, into use, it can lift us out
of all kinds of limitation.

A statement I have used many times over
the years, one that has helped lift me out of
limitation, is this: *"Christ in me now frees me
from all limitation. I am the resurrection and
the life."*

Paul said that this resurrected Christ nature in man is the mystery that has been hid for

generations, and he described it as man's hope of glory. He reminded the early Christians of their divinity: "Do you not know that your body is a temple of the Holy Spirit within you, which you have from God? . . . So glorify God in your body."

Charles Fillmore described resurrection as the "raising up of the whole man—spirit, soul, and body—into the Christ consciousness of life and wholeness." He wrote in *Keep a True Lent:*

"The time is ripe for the advent of a new race, the advent of the spiritualized man. This will be brought about not by a miracle or the fiat of God, but by the gradual refinement of the man of the flesh into the man of Spirit. The true overcomer is qualifying himself to become a member of the new spiritualized race."

Just as Jesus, through His resurrection of His spiritual nature, brought back into notice this spiritualized man, so we can bring alive the divinity within us, and in other people. As we do, we become a part of the spiritualized race which overcomes or "comes up over" the negative experiences of life.

"Think of yourself in a large way, and the little things of life will lose interest for you," says Charles Fillmore. "See all things from the large viewpoint. Instead of seeing yourself as mere man, see yourself as divine being. The only difference between gods and men is in comprehension. Men have the power to comprehend and appropriate all they have imagined possible with God."

From a practical standpoint, you can see yourself and others in a large way, as divine beings, through praise. Praise is one of the strongest forms of love. Praise expands your good. Praise is your resurrecting power because it brings back into notice and use, back to life, the good in yourself and in others. Ella Wheeler Wilcox was expressing the highest form of praise in her poem "Attainment" when she wrote,

> "Know that you are great,
> Great with divinity."

The word *praise* means to express approval, to glorify, to appraise as good. When you express approval of yourself or others, you are glorifying the divine in yourself and others. Always you can resurrect or bring back to notice the good, the divinity in people and situations through praise.

Say to yourself often: *"Through the power of Christ within me, I can be as wonderful as I want to be!"* Whether it seems to be literally true or not, begin to think of yourself as glorious, splendid, beloved, strong, well, capable. Begin to think of the world as a beautiful place in which to live, work, grow, play. Affirm often for others, especially those who trouble you: *"Through the power of Christ within you, you can be as wonderful as you want to be!"* You will be surprised how this simple, delightful way of thinking will resurrect—bring back to notice, restore to life—your good. Also, declare often for any situation that troubles you: *"I appraise this situation as good."*

I once knew of an employer for whom no one liked to work. This solemn, serious man was irritable, impatient, hard to please. One bookkeeper who had worked for him for many years finally had to resign because of ill health. Everyone wondered what would become of the employer, since nobody wanted the bookkeeper's job. None of the local townspeople applied for it.

Instead, an out-of-town bookkeeper took the job. She was a happy, jolly, attractive person, quite in contrast to the serious, drab, complaining person who had previously worked for this man. She obviously expected to have a good time in her new job. She was appraising the situation as good.

She planned each day around her new employer's well-being. She came in early to beautify his office and set things in order before beginning the day. She often brought fresh flowers for his desk from her garden. She inquired about how he wanted everything done and made it a point to please him. She often complimented him on some aspect of his work, or perhaps on his wife and family. By making things as pleasant as possible, the bookkeeper slowly transformed her employer into a calm, peaceful, happy individual.

For the first time in years, he smiled regularly and genuinely. It was a joy to those about him to observe him so happy and relaxed. In his appreciation he loosened his purse strings and gave the new employee several raises. Soon she was making more money than his previous bookkeeper had made. This happy state of affairs continued for some time until the bookkeeper's husband was transferred to an out-of-state position, and she left her job to join him. On her last day in the office, her boss actually cried softly. He held a luncheon in her honor and gave her a substantial bonus check as a going-away gift.

The next bookkeeper who came to work for this man knew nothing of appraising people and situations as good, thereby resurrecting the good in them. She knew nothing of the magic power of praise and approval. The result was that the employer retreated into his shell of unpleasantness and soon regained his title of many years' standing as the hardest man in town to work for.

In this season, when you see beauty, life, pleasantness springing up all around in the wonders of nature, use often the resurrecting power of love through praise. Express approval of others, appraise situations as good regardless of appearances, and glorify your own appearance and your world. As you do so, you will become a part of the resurrecting power of love that is mightily at work in every atom of the universe.

You can glorify your own appearance and that of your world by creating as much beauty as possible. A famous actress was once asked how she stayed so young, though she was actually past seventy. Her reply was that she remained youthful by looking at beauty, appreciating beauty, thinking about beauty.

You can have more beauty in your world if you will begin right where you are to add whatever touches of beauty are possible. As you do this, beauty will multiply in your life. As you dwell more and more on beauty and do all that is possible to produce it in your world, you will become more successful and prosperous.

Once I found myself in a situation where there seemed to be no beauty. One room looked especially hopeless. It was a hopeless clutter of old, worn-out, discarded furniture. A friend who knew of the resurrecting power of beauty kept looking at that cluttered room too. We could not decide what possible use could be made of it, for it seemed so unsightly. Finally we decided to "form a vacuum" by getting rid of all the old furniture, drapes, and rugs.

Almost immediately after the room was emptied, ideas began to come for its redecoration. As the ideas came, we were able to find one item that fitted our redecoration theme. We bought that piece and placed it in the empty room. That one beautiful object was like a magnet. It quickly drew other beautiful objects, as gifts. Money came easily for more costly items to create an elegant atmosphere. Everything and everybody seemed to want to enhance the beauty of that room. Soon it was the most beautiful room in the entire building. People often visited that room just to feed on its beauty. They said that it gave them a sense of peace, serenity, well-being. Soon the essence of beauty in that room seemed to permeate the entire building, and redecoration of other rooms took place.

You can use this method for building a beautiful wardrobe of clothes, or for furnishing your home or office. Begin by getting one truly elegant item that delights you and makes you feel rich. If it is an item of clothing, wear it often, mentally appreciating it, and it will open the way for other lovely clothes to be yours.

By fixing your attention on one beautiful item, you create the mental image of beauty, and that image goes to work through you and through others to create more beauty for you. The important thing is to make a start toward beauty, even in a small way. As you do, beauty multiplies for you, and you are able to resurrect beauty and to glorify your life and your world.

Beauty also has resurrecting power for health. When you are trying to achieve freedom from aches and pains, that is the time to wear your brightest, light-colored clothes. The body seems to respond to bright, light colors that suggest life, health, vitality.

Color-healing is an ancient science that is now being rediscovered. It was practiced in the healing temples of ancient Egypt, India, and China. Experiments have recently been made in some of our modern hospitals to learn the effect of color on a patient's recovery. Particularly in mental hospitals is color therapy known to be effective.

A schoolteacher, following an automobile accident, broke out with a painful rash which medical treatment failed to alleviate. It was suggested that she begin giving thanks for the perfect healing in a joyous, happy manner, and that she wear her prettiest, brightest clothes every day until she was healed. It was suggested that instead of staying home and trying to hide the rash, she should get into a party mood and have a good time. It sounded like a ridiculous prescription for healing. But it worked.

A woman who had suffered for months with various aches and pains found that neither medical nor metaphysical treatment seemed to help, until it was suggested that she stop wearing the dark clothes she had worn for months. As she put on light, bright-colored clothes, her body seemed to rejoice in being clothed in beauty, and her aches and pains faded away. She also looked younger, and this helped her mentally to accept a perfect healing. An appropriate affirmation for this purpose is, *"I pour out upon my body temple the oil of love and clothe it in garments of praise."*

Another way to glorify your divinity and resurrect your good is through joy. Emma Curtis Hopkins has described the resurrecting power of joy. "Exaltation is a magnet for all good things of the universe to hasten to you. Depression and anxiety are a magnet for trouble to fly to you. . . . There is no power of healing in a depressed state of mind. . . . In order to work your best, metaphysically, you must be in an exalted state of mind."

A woman who had experienced great sorrow in her life gave in to despondency, insomnia, and depression. Finally her physician informed her that she would have to overcome her depression, which was affecting her health. He advised her that the way to conquer depression was to laugh at least three times a day, whether she felt like it or not.

Though it seemed ridiculous to follow this advice, she began retiring to her room three times daily for the sole purpose of laughing and making merry, whether there was actually anything to laugh about or not. She was soon in excellent health again, and her previously sorrowful life took on a happy new look.

Charles Fillmore has written: "All healing systems recognize joy as a beneficent factor in the restoration of health to the sick. . . . That there is an intimate relation between happiness and health goes without question."

A business executive had a sudden attack of acute indigestion. He decided to see if joy would heal him. He had heard a lecturer say, "If you can manage to smile continuously for just five minutes, you can cure any pain." He went to the mirror and stood there smiling, timing himself by his watch to be sure he held the smile for five minutes. By the end of the five minutes, he was so amused at this method that he was laughing aloud. Suddenly he thought of the acute pain he had experienced just five minutes earlier. It was gone!

Fun, laughter, and joy are among the world's cheapest and best medicines. Give yourself large doses of these often. They will not only save you expensive medical bills, they will make your body healthier and your life happier.

If a person does not know of the resurrecting power of maintaining a joyous, pleasant frame of mind, someone near him can still help resurrect his good by maintaining a joyous attitude about his life and affairs.

A popular radio announcer was warned that he would die of cancer. When the doctors told his wife that he had cancer and could not possibly live, she replied: "Tell me no more. I refuse to accept that diagnosis. My husband is too fine a man to die. He still has so much to give the world. I have faith that my husband is going to be healed." She continued to maintain this pleasant, faith-filled attitude.

Not only did the man have cancer; he was also an alcoholic. When relatives and friends had tried earlier to console his wife about his drinking, she had not accepted their sympathy. Instead she had replied: "My husband is too fine a man to be addicted to alcohol. He is going to be healed."

When her husband was sent home from the hospital, his case diagnosed as hopeless, he and his wife joined a prayer group that believed in spiritual healing. Many of his radio listeners were also praying for his healing. Through consistent prayer, he was healed of cancer and also of the desire to drink.

A famous television personality learned of the announcer's healing of cancer. Since the television star had recently had an operation for cancer and his future seemed uncertain, he wrote the announcer asking his secret for having made such a successful comeback. The announcer wrote back: "In the first place, don't believe any diagnosis you are given, unless you are told you can be healed. Refuse to believe anything else. Then pray daily, asking God what it is in life you are really supposed to do, and *joyously* get busy doing it!"

This series of events took place several years ago. Both the radio announcer and the television personality are still well and active in their careers.

Lowell Fillmore has described the resurrecting power of joyous, happy words:

"Good words taken into our mouth bring happiness and prosperity into our life, while . . . angry words interfere with the digestive processes in our stomach and upset other functions of our body. When you give someone a good tongue-lashing you harm yourself more than you do your target. . . . There is no nourishment in words of criticism concerning evil. . . . Neither can you grow and prosper on hard words. . . . Let your conversation be composed of words that are filled with the constructive vitamins of Spirit. . . . So when you have anything to say, say it for goodness' sake."

Just as nature is coming alive at this season through the expression of beauty and joy, you can bring back to notice, to use, to life the divinity within you through the expression of beauty and joy. Express the resurrecting power of love often by affirming: *"Through the power of Christ within me, I can be as wonderful as I want to be! I pour out upon my body temple the oil of love and clothe it in garments of praise. I appraise my mind, body, and affairs as good. I appraise others as good as I affirm for them: 'Through the power of Christ in you, you can be as wonderful as you want to be.' I say it for goodness' sake. And I give thanks that we are all great—great with divinity!"*

A Special Method of Love

IT IS ONE of the basic teachings of Truth that all environments, circumstances, and conditions that we experience existed first as ideas in our own mind. One of the great secrets of love is to learn how to clear inharmonious ideas from our own consciousness, for this in turn clears inharmonious experiences and relationships from our life. If you deal in the right way with your own thinking, the people around you will move into right conditions—either in your midst or by moving out of your life. In one way or another, harmony will be established.

I want to share with you a special method

for getting your thinking into divine order, promptly and surely.

You can employ this special method of love secretly—with words. True words are angels. True words are alive with good, and they produce good. But there is a definite method by which you can employ words and produce angelic results: by thinking of the person you are concerned about as having an angel or higher self (Christ self), to whom you write.

By writing to a person's angel, you establish in your own thinking a harmonious belief about that person; you radiate your harmonious feeling to that person subconsciously; and you also recognize and bring alive in that person's consciousness his own higher, spiritual self.

There is special power in writing to the angel of a person whom you cannot reason with or help in the usual ways. There is something about written words of Truth that reaches to the judgment seat of such a person, getting past the emotional blocks of vanity, pride, deception, intellectual arguments, and penetrating his God-self.

All religions and cultures have taught that a man's word is his power. Many teachings have realized the special power of written words. The Chinese have such an affection for the written word that they have been taught for centuries never to tear up a sheet of writing, nor to misuse any paper with written words on it, even if it has no further practical use. The Greeks have long believed that words are filled with cosmic power; that one can do anything with words, build or destroy.

John, in his Revelation, speaks of writing to the angels of the seven churches. The word *church* symbolizes spiritual consciousness. The seven churches are symbolic of the seven types of people whom we can reach spiritually by writing to their angels, when we seem unable to reach them in other ways.

I have known a number of persons who have used this special method of love for reaching troublesome people and clearing up inharmony. A young doctor recently learned of this method. For some months he had been out of harmony with another doctor and had used every means he knew to restore harmony, but the other physician had rebuffed his bids for reconciliation. The young doctor began writing daily to the angel of the other man, asking that perfect understanding be re-established between them. Later the other doctor met him on the street, greeted him graciously, and invited him to lunch. Now they are again good friends.

There are seven types of people you can reach by writing to their angels.

"To the angel of the church in Ephesus write"

The word *Ephesus* means "desirable, appealing." You may know appealing people who are hard to reach. Their outward life is full of excitement. They are emotional, lovers of amusement, theatrical in their tastes, dramatic in everything they do. Paul spent three years preaching Truth in Ephesus, because he realized such people were hard to reach and help.

The wonderful thing to remember about those whom you are trying to help in this category is that they have an intense desire for greater good in their lives. Though they seem unsettled, they are easy to know, pleasant and agreeable, and they are interested in the finer things of life. By writing to their angels, stating the Truth about them, you easily reach that deeper phase of their nature, and they happily respond.

I once knew a fine person of this type. His outer life was full of excitement. He was emotional, a lover of amusement, theatrical in his tastes, and dramatic in everything he did. He owed me for some work I had done for his firm. Several months had passed and I had not been paid. My affirmations had not brought results.

Finally I remembered the angel-writing technique, and one night (quite late) I quietly wrote: *"To the angel of* (let us say) *John Brown, I bless you and give thanks that you are handling this financial matter promptly, and that I am immediately and completely paid."* (I wrote this statement fifteen times, because many mystics believe that fifteen is the number that dissolves adversity and hard conditions.)

After writing out the statement, I felt much better about the situation and was able to release it completely from my mind. Two days later, my friend telephoned to say his bookkeeper was writing my check and that I would receive it by mail the following day—and I did!

"And to the angel of the church in Smyrna write"

The word *Smyrna* means "flowing substance." Smyrnians make a fine appearance. They are lovers of show, beauty, adornment. They live beyond their means and usually have financial problems.

A businessman was having great difficulty with his wife, who had divorced him. He was heartbroken because he still loved her. He had tried to talk with her about reconciliation, but she was very confused, and he could not reason with her.

He learned of this special method of love and was fascinated with the idea, realizing that his wife was this second type. She made a fine appearance and was a lover of show and beauty. In fact, that had been one of their basic problems: her tastes had been much too expensive for his pocketbook.

He began writing each night to her angel, asking help in straightening out their marriage. One day, after he had not heard from her for some time, she contacted him, tearfully declaring that their divorce had been a mistake. Soon they were remarried. This man has found it possible to maintain peace and harmony with his wife by continuing to write to her angel.

"And to the angel of the church in Pergamum write"

The word *Pergamum* means "strongly united, closely knit." This is the grand, often wealthy, aristocratic type—literary, scientific, artistic, lovers of society and statescraft, strongly united, closely knit in family, social, and business relationships. These persons may be suspicious of strangers, new friends, new ideas.

A young man fell in love and wanted to marry. But the girl of his choice was from a close-knit family that did not want to release her emotionally. This family group was suspicious of new people, new ways of doing things, all new ideas. In fact, they were strongly united against the invasion of anything new in their lives.

The young man realized that from a human standpoint, it seemed hopeless to try to win the girl, even though she was in love with him, because of her strong family ties. Being a Truth student, he reasoned that the only possible way to deal with the possessiveness of her family was through the practice of love.

It was at this point that he learned of love's special method. He wrote to the girl's angel and to the angel of her family, decreeing for her emotional freedom, a happy marriage, and a family divinely adjusted to this change. For some months, he continued this angel-writing technique, with no visible results. Then suddenly everything changed. He could sense a freedom that had not previously existed. He proposed, and they were soon married. Though it took her family some time to adjust to the change and to accept him emotionally into the family, they finally did so wholeheartedly.

"And to the angel of the church in Thyatira write"

Thyatira means "rushing headlong, frantic, zealous, quarrelsome, easily offended." People of this type have greater ideals than inner ability for producing idealistic results. Thyatirans are quite often interested in athletics.

A housewife learned that the instructor at a health club was being harsh with the teen-age boys he was instructing. Though her son and his friends were upset by this harsh treatment, they did not wish her to interfere, feeling that would bring only more scorn from their instructor. The mother asked the boys to begin writing to the angel of their instructor, decreeing fair treatment and understanding. She joined them in their angel-writing project.

For a time no results were apparent. Suddenly, however, the instructor announced he was leaving his job to take a better position with a local college. Along with an increased income, the new job would allow him time to work on his master's degree, which had long been his desire. The mother then realized that the young instructor's harsh treatment apparently had stemmed from his own frustration and job dissatisfaction. The amazing result was that this woman's son later won a trophy from the health club—a trophy topped with the figure of an angel!

"And to the angel of the church in Sardis write"

The word *Sardis* means "prince of power, timid, apprehensive, always fearful about something." These people are body devotees. They are afraid of drafts, accidents, what they eat. They are always seeking the comfortable, soft, pleasant things of bodily life. No books, lessons, or instructions seem to quench their fears, but writing to their angels uplifts the bold, brave, dauntless spirit in them, and they become "princes of power."

This type of person is always changing his mind. The throat, which is the power center in the body, is usually a weak spot. He may develop a sore throat or some other throat ailment when he becomes fearful.

Such a person has great potential for becoming a powerful individual. You awaken that power center within him and bring it alive through writing to his angel. This gives him a stability and fearlessness that he desires to express.

A man was once having difficulty trying to bring a business matter to a conclusion. It had been pending for a long time. Everyone involved was congenial and wished to conclude negotiations except one man, who kept changing his mind. He seemed unsure about every aspect of the matter.

The businessman heard of the angel-writing method and realized that the man who kept changing his mind was timid, apprehensive, fearful, unsure. He wrote to the man's angel, asking that the business matter be brought to an early, appropriate conclusion, so that all involved would be satisfied and blessed.

A few days later, the man who had stalled for so long said, "Come down to my office tomorrow morning and the papers will be ready to sign." Then he added, as though it were his idea, "This situation has been delayed long enough, and I am anxious to conclude it."

"And to the angel of the church in Philadelphia write"

The word *Philadelphia* means "brotherly love, fraternal love, universal love." People of this type talk much about the brotherhood of man, but love to them means outer works alone, rather than an inner consciousness of love. These are the philanthropists of human existence. Community organizations, clubs, fraternal groups, civic groups, churches are all filled with people seeking brotherly love, universal love. They sometimes become frustrated through exhausting themselves in loving works.

If you find yourself in a group or organization where the loving works do not seem to be balanced by an inner consciousness of love, you can write to the angel of that organization, asking that divine love come alive in the thoughts as well as in the actions of the group. As you do, those people who are not in tune with divine love will fade harmoniously out of the group, and those who are lovingly in tune with its aims and purposes will appear. In this secret, quiet way both inner and outer harmony can be established and maintained.

An executive found himself in the midst of organizational inharmony. He was not sure just who was responsible for the unrest and critical attitudes found in the group. He tried various methods for re-establishing harmony, but the group remained aloof, critical, inharmonious.

In desperation, he began writing daily to the angel of that organization, asking for help in re-establishing a consciousness of love. Then he wrote: "I cast this burden on the angel of divine love. The angel of love now comes alive in this situation and in all persons connected with this organization. The angel of divine love now reigns supreme."

Soon several volunteer workers resigned their jobs, leaving the organization, and new workers appeared who were eager to contribute to the progress of the organization in a harmonious way. Peace and progress were established and maintained.

"And to the angel of the church in Laodicea write"

The word *Laodicea* means "justice and judgment." People of this type often have an injustice complex. They are unstable, unsettled, changeable, wanderers seeking new doctrines and new places. They often change their re-

ligious beliefs and their political views. They
are restless, critical. They often feel that they
have been wronged or misused.

You find this type of person going from one
job to another; from one church to another;
from one club to another. They are the "joiners"
who do not remain with anything long enough
to discover whether it will benefit them or not.

When you write to the angel of such a person, decree that the divine law of love and
justice is doing its perfect work in his life and
affairs, and that he is being divinely guided into
his right place. He will subconsciously respond
more and more to your high vision of rightness
and stability for him.

In writing to another's angel, it may appear
that nothing is being accomplished. Then, suddenly, everything will shift, changes will come,
and matters that had seemed destined for failure
will clear up very quickly.

The word *angel* means "messenger of God."
Do not fail to write to your own angel when it
seems that your life is filled with defeat, or when
you are tempted to criticize and condemn yourself. *The Metaphysical Bible Dictionary* ex-
plains: "The office of the angels is to guard and
guide and direct the natural forces of mind and
body, which have in them the future of the
whole man."

Emma Curtis Hopkins writes: "The Angel of His Presence accompanies every man. . . . This high leadership is every man's heritage. He need not fear dangerous days or vicious circumstances while he is aware that his angel goes before him, pleads his cause and defends him."

When challenges arise, say to yourself: "I have nothing to fear. My guardian angel goes before me, making right my way." Decree it for others. A businesswoman was concerned about having to make an out-of-town buying trip, which required that she drive two hundred miles in rain and fog, accompanied by her ailing husband, whom she could not leave at home alone. A friend said, "You have nothing to fear, because your guardian angel will be with you."

Upon returning from the buying trip, she said to her friend: "It *did* seem that we were accompanied by an angel. As I drove out of town, within a few minutes the sky cleared of fog, the rain stopped, and the sun shone through. There was no more bad weather on the entire trip. The drive helped my husband's spirits and he suffered no ill effects from it. Financially, this proved to be the most profitable buying trip I have made in a long time."

Never expect your angel or that of another to honor any requests that might hurt or harm.

Be willing that something infinitely better than that which you tentatively want shall come as you use love's special method. This will open the way for your good and for the good of all involved to manifest in an unlimited, satisfying manner.

For invoking love's special method, meditate often upon the promise of the Psalmist: "No evil shall befall you,

No scourge come near your tent.

For he will give his angels charge of you,

To guard you in all your ways."

Prosperity Is Divinely Approved (I)

An analyst recently stated that he had found that one of the greatest causes of failure in people is confused thought about whether success is divinely approved or condemned. Many of the business people he treats express the belief that failure is spiritually approved, rather than success, citing the words of Jesus, "You cannot serve God and mammon." This doctor says he has spent many an hour explaining to his patients that being success-minded is not serving mammon, and that they should stop using God as an excuse for their failures. The dictionary defines mammon as "the demon of cupidity." Serving mammon means leaving God out of one's financial affairs and trying to succeed alone, through purely human methods.

God pointed out the right spiritual attitude toward prosperity when He instructed Moses to remind the Children of Israel: "You shall remember the Lord your God, for it is he who gives you power to get wealth." One definition of the word *wealth* is "well-being." That is what man should be working toward and should expect as his spiritual heritage.

What a difference it can make in a person's life to realize that prosperity is divinely approved! A businesswoman was having difficulties in every phase of her life. She had a good income but it seemed to dissipate very rapidly and she had little to show for it. She was unable to get along with her co-workers; she was involved in a lawsuit in connection with her previous job; her doctor warned that she was on the brink of a nervous breakdown; her husband had left her, and her teen-age children seemed to have turned against her.

One night a friend invited her to attend a prosperity lecture. That was the turning point in her life. She learned that prosperity and success are divinely approved; that prosperity is the peace, health, and plenty of a balanced way of life; that it begins with prosperous, successful, unlimited attitudes. As she began to dwell on the goodness of God and man, she began to experience a sense of peace such as she had not known for a long time.

As her attitudes changed, so did her way of life. In due time, her husband returned home; she was gradually able to establish a more harmonious relationship with her children; she did not have a nervous collapse; the lawsuit regarding her former job was quietly and amicably settled out of court; and she was able to get along well with her co-workers and find joy and satisfaction in her work. Indeed, she reflected a transformed attitude and a transformed appearance.

A certain businessman had been a failure for years because subconsciously he felt guilty about succeeding. He had been reared in a family that considered poverty a spiritual virtue. As he grew up, he began to realize that poverty cannot possibly be a virtue because it causes so much of the world's troubles. He saw that poverty fills prisons with thieves and murderers, drives men and women to degradation and despair. He realized that poverty drives potentially fine, talented, intelligent children to delinquency and crime; that poverty often makes people do things they otherwise would never think of doing.

Nevertheless, this man never fully succeeded in business until he learned of the power of prosperous thinking. Finally he was convinced that prosperity is divinely approved, and that he should deliberately and definitely expect prosperity as a spiritual blessing. From that point on, his whole life was changed. Previous business failure and heavy indebtedness are now being dissolved through the rich ideas he is receiving as a result of deliberate, prosperous thinking. Often he meditates upon this statement: *"Rich, appropriate, divine ideas now come to me from every direction, and I wisely use them now."*

Stop feeling guilty about wanting to be prosperous. Instead, begin to study the Bible as a great prosperity textbook. You will be amazed and delighted by the prosperity techniques it will unfold to you.

For instance, the first chapter of Genesis emphasizes the power there is in speaking definite words that will produce definite results. "Let there be" is God's prosperity decree. It is interesting to note that all ancient scriptures stress this prosperity secret, the power of spoken words for creating desired good.

Dr. H. Emilie Cady, a homeopathic physician in New York City for many years, relates in *How I Used Truth* how she discovered the prospering power there is in spoken words.

For several years she tried to demonstrate prosperity in her practice on a free-will-offering basis, because of the great financial need of many of her patients in those days. For two years she worked at this prosperity arrangement. Though she had felt strongly guided to try it, it was not working out. One day, in desperation, she asked further divine guidance in the matter; and the answer that came was from the first chapter of Genesis, "God said, Let there be light: and there was light." She kept repeating over and over the words *"God said."* This helped her to see that she must speak words for prosperity. She began to think of the words of John in describing the creation story: "In the beginning was the Word . . . and without him [the Word] was not anything made that was made."

She writes: "That was all I needed. I saw plainly that while I had, for two years, hopefully and happily gone on enduring hardships, believing that God would supply, I had not once spoken the word *'It is done: God is now manifested as my supply.'* Believe me, that day I spoke the word of my deliverance. Suffice it to say that the supply problem was ended that day for all time and has never entered my life or mind since."

A wealthy woman has told how she used prosperous decrees during the depression years when her husband's business was being challenged. She gathered together her children daily, to sit for some time and speak definite prosperity affirmations for the business. Often they declared: *"Large sums of money now come into the business in God's own wonderful way."* Often they decreed the words of the Psalmist: *"Send now prosperity."* And paraphrasing the decrees of Genesis, they affirmed: *"Let there be abundant supply, and let it come forth now with the ease, speed, and wisdom of Spirit."*

While this woman's neighbors talked lack, she affirmed abundance. While they held tightly to their money, she blessed her pocketbook, bank account, and financial affairs. She dared to invoke the law of receiving by spending her money fearlessly. When she made a financial transaction, she would think of her larger bills as being broken down into smaller denominations and going forth, blessed, to be multiplied and to return in multiplied amounts. To keep fear and limited ideas from creeping in, she decreed as she paid her bills: *"I exercise wisdom and good judgment, and all my affairs are prospered."*

This woman's husband prospered all through the depression years; later he acquired considerable wealth. As for the children, who joined in those prosperity prayers, they are now married with families of their own; all of them are exceedingly prosperous young adults. They have already achieved greater prosperity than many persons do in their entire lifetime, in the same fields of work.

Never hesitate to pray definitely for prosperity; to decree definite words for prosperity; to image and expect prosperous results. This prosperity secret is the universal wisdom of the ages for prosperous living. Indeed, the history of mankind shows that the first prayers of primitive man were prosperity prayers for clothing, shelter, and food. In reality, primitive man decreed the words of the Psalmist, "Send now prosperity."

The great men of the Bible were rich from birth, became prosperous later on, or at least had access to riches whenever a need arose. Abraham, the father of the Hebrew nation, became "very rich in cattle, in silver, and in gold." The Hebrews at that time had close contact with the Babylonians, apparently borrowing certain traditions from them and using these as a basis for their own way of life. Among the traditions carried over from the wealthy Babylonians was the prosperity law of tithing.

The first instance of tithing related in the Bible was when Abraham gave a "tenth of all"

to Melchizedek, king of Salem, declaring, "I
have sworn to the Lord God Most High, maker
of heaven and earth, that I would not take a
thread or a sandal-thong or anything that is
yours, lest you should say, 'I have made Abram
rich.' " As though promising Abraham both protection and prosperity for his act of tithing, the
Scriptural account continues: "After these things
the word of the Lord came to Abram in a vision,
'Fear not, Abram, I am your shield; your reward
shall be very great.' "

Tithing is a powerful prosperity principle
because it causes the tither to invoke the basic
law of prosperity: giving and receiving. In
modern times we have heard the term "giving
and receiving" so often that we may be inclined
to discount its importance. But in ancient Egypt,
the prosperity law of giving and receiving was
considered so powerful that it was a secret teaching, given only to the privileged few, as were
all the Hermetic principles. In fact, the law of
giving and receiving was considered such a
powerful law that the Egyptian rulers dared not
share it with the masses, if they wished to continue controlling them. In some ways, the law is
still a "secret" teaching, because most people today do not fully understand its power for prosperity and achievement.

Sometimes persons of moderate means feel

that it would be a hardship to begin tithing, and dismiss it as a practice for the rich. However, the consistent practice of tithing is a means of establishing anyone in a consciousness of consistent giving, which opens the way to consistent receiving. One businessman says that he *had* to tithe, to get out of debt and stay out of debt! A businesswoman was asked, "What do you think of tithing?" She replied, "Why, if I didn't tithe I'd be picked as clean as a bird. I've got to tithe to keep going." It has often been said, "You'll never find a tither in the poorhouse."

Richard Lynch has written: "An expansion of consciousness results from the grace of giving in the right spirit. We all have seen instances of shriveled souls, directly due to financial grasping and withholding. Physical inharmony, such as paralysis, often results from this state of mind. . . .

"The popular mind doubts that prosperity will come through giving up a tithe of all financial receipts. I should like to call attention to this actuality: The world's richest man [Rockefeller] tells us that he willingly tithes his income, which, you may imagine, is no small amount of money. He considers it one of the greatest blessings of life that he was taught, when a lad of eight years and earning only ten cents a day, to give away regularly a portion of his income to purposes of public and religious character."

A close study of Abraham's life reveals several other prosperity secrets. His grandson Jacob followed the practice of tithing and became a very prosperous man. Jacob also used a method well known to the ancients for producing satisfying results—that of making a covenant with the Lord.

In his covenant, Jacob asked for divine protection, for food, clothing, shelter, work, and harmony in his family relationships. In return for these blessings he covenanted to tithe all that he received. His resulting prosperity is thus described: "The man Jacob became rich, and gained more and more until he became very wealthy. He had possessions of flocks and herds, and a great household." Later he was reconciled with his brother Esau, whom he had earlier deceived. The extent of his prosperity is shown in the rich reconciliation gift he gave Esau: "Two hundred she-goats and twenty he-goats, two hundred ewes and twenty rams, thirty milch camels and their colts, forty cows and ten bulls, twenty she-asses and ten foals." He presented these to Esau with these words: "Accept, I pray you, my gift that is brought to you; because God has dealt graciously with me, and because I have enough."

In modern times, many have found it wise to follow Jacob's ancient prosperity method of making a covenant with God. One young woman had been in ill health, was out of harmony with her family, and was unable to obtain suitable work, though she held a master's degree in her field. She heard of Jacob's method and wrote out her covenant, asking for divine guidance about her life work, decreeing harmony with her parents (who had long attempted to dominate her), and affirming restored mental and physical health. In return, she promised to give faithfully a "tenth of all" that she received.

Almost immediately a satisfying job opened up for her. Soon her health, both mental and physical, began to improve. In due time, her parents became more understanding and seemed to release her emotionally to find her own way in life. It was only after these results appeared that she divulged her success technique of writing out a definite covenant with God, including her practice of tithing.

Joseph has been described by historians as the "successful businessman of the Old Testament," because of his foresight that saved Egypt from a seven-year famine that affected the rest of the ancient world. Note the emphasis placed upon rich apparel in the story of Joseph: On the day that he rose from obscurity and long im-

prisonment to become prime minister of Egypt,
Pharaoh put a signet ring on Joseph's finger, ar-
rayed him in fine linens, placed a gold chain
about his neck, and insisted that he ride in the
second chariot, next in importance to his own.

The importance of good apparel is emphasized in a number of instances in the Bible.
Moses, the great emancipator of the Hebrews,
was reared as a prince in the household of
Pharaoh. As the adopted son of Pharaoh's
daughter, he went about in fine garments, lived
like a young gentleman, and was provided with
a royal education.

God gave Moses specific instructions concerning the rich garments his brother Aaron was
to wear as Israel's first high priest. These garments were to be made of fine linen in brilliant
colors set in gold, worn with emeralds, dia-
monds, and other precious stones. All of God's
children should have the advantages of rich
apparel and beautiful environments.

Charles Fillmore pointed out that the familiar parable of the prodigal son is in reality
a prosperity parable, emphasizing the fact that
the prosperous person should wear good clothes.
Concerning the statement, "Bring forth quickly
the best robe and put it on him," Mr. Fillmore
writes: "That was a lesson in good apparel. It is
a sin to wear poor clothes . . . The next act of the

father was to put a gold ring on the prodigal's finger, another evidence of prosperity. The Father's desire for us is unlimited good, not merely the means of a meager existence."

David decreed a prosperous environment:

"Peace be within your walls,
and security within your towers."

A favorite affirmation of mine for demonstrating a beautiful environment has been: *"I have a divine right to the best, and I now trust my divine rights to bring me out right in experiencing the best."* The daily use of this statement helped produce a beautiful new home. As I continued to affirm these words, the way opened for the purchase of beautiful furniture, lovely drapes, and appropriate electrical appliances for the home. Gifts of china, silver, crystal, linens, and kitchen utensils came to me. It was then that I began to feel the need for a housekeeper to help maintain the lovely new house. One day a friend telephoned to say that a very competent maid of her acquaintance, whom I had met previously, had said that she wanted to become my housekeeper.

Several years later, when I married and came to the Southwest to live, again I began to use that statement: *"I have a divine right to the best, and I now trust my divine rights to bring me out right in experiencing the best."* This time my husband and I were looking for an apartment convenient to the University of Texas, where he taught. Since we had been traveling all summer and had arrived in town only a few days before school began, it seemed by human standards utterly impossible to find a suitable unfurnished apartment that would meet our needs, within walking distance of the university campus. Nevertheless, we decreed what we wanted, declaring in detail just the type of apartment desired.

Shortly an ad appeared in the paper. We investigated it, and it proved to be the answer to all our decrees for "the best." The apartment was spacious, had just been redecorated, and was within sight of the university! The colors in which it had been redecorated perfectly matched our furniture. Furthermore, the rental price of this apartment, we discovered, was more reasonable than that of any others in the surrounding area. As we continued affirming our right to the best, a housekeeper appeared who had long worked in the building, and asked to work for us. Whenever people complain about "how hard it is to find good help," I think of how this affirmation for "the best" brought me competent help when I needed it.

When you are trying to expand your mental acceptance of beautiful surroundings and rich supply, it is good to study the life of David's son Solomon. Historians state that during his forty-year rule, Solomon "spent money like water." The temple he built cost untold millions. He lived on a grand scale in his palace, eating from dishes made of solid gold. "And Solomon's provision for one day was thirty cors of fine flour, and sixty cors of meal, ten fat oxen, and twenty pasture-fed cattle, a hundred sheep, besides harts, gazelles, roebucks, and fatted fowl."

The prosperity prayer Solomon used early in his life became the foundation of his wealth: "Give thy servant therefore an understanding mind, to govern thy people, that I may discern between good and evil." Charles Fillmore has written: "King Solomon was probably the world's richest man, and in so far as the world is concerned he was a great success. He demonstrated prosperity. He did not ask God for riches. Let us note that carefully. He asked God for wisdom, for ideas. God is mind and His gifts are not material but spiritual, not things but ideas. Solomon asked for and received the ideas and then developed them himself. Because he was wise all the world came to his court seeking wisdom and bringing riches in exchange for it. The King of Tyre brought the material he needed to build the Temple. The Queen of

Sheba brought him great quantities of gold. From this we should get our cue: ask God for rich ideas (substance) and then put them to work in our affairs."

A businessman who read *Working with God,* by Gardner Hunting, was struck forcibly by these words: "Inspiration—your own creative urge—waits in your heart, and it will transform your life, your career, your happiness, your prosperity if you will only listen and let it." This man was greatly inspired by the author's emphasis upon ideas as channels of supply. One night he had a dream in which an invention was revealed to him. He developed that invention, and became a multimillionaire. When anyone asks the secret of this man's success, he gives the inquirer a copy of *Working with God.* He has become an active member of his local Unity center and has contributed generously to it in rich appreciation for what the Unity message of prosperity has meant to him.

Always when you have a problem, if you will ask for divine ideas to discern between the true and the false in the situation, you will be guided to a solution. A housewife once asked how she could help her husband realize greater prosperity. He was in the real-estate business and had not been able to sell a house for a number of weeks. It was suggested that she should quietly affirm that her husband was being endowed with "divine ideas and divine activity." She did, and things began to happen for him. Within two days he sold a house; within a few more days, he sold a second house. These transactions gave him the emotional as well as financial lift needed to bring his business affairs out of a slump and to begin selling consistently again.

Many of the Old Testament prophets were prosperous or had access to riches. One of the most outstanding, Isaiah, belonged to the aristocratic class in Jerusalem and may have been a member of the royal family. His voice was heard and heeded in high places, and his position doubtless helped to lend weight to his words.

Elisha fully appreciated the mental and spiritual laws of prosperity, using them to multiply the widow's oil, so that she might pay her debts and live comfortably. Charles Fillmore has written of this prosperity story: "Change your thought and increase your substance in the mind, as Elisha increased the oil for the widow. Get larger receptacles and plenty of them. Even a very small idea of substance may be added to and increased. The widow had a very small amount of oil, but as the prophet blessed it, it increased until it filled every vessel she could borrow from the neighbors. We should form the habit of blessing everything that we have. It may seem foolish to some persons that we bless our nickels, dimes, and dollars, but we know that we are setting the law of increase in operation . . . Elisha used a small amount of oil to produce a great amount of—oil. So when we bless our money or other goods, we are complying with a divine law of increase that has been demonstrated many times."

Elijah, who had been Elisha's master and teacher, was greatly interested in the prosperity of the Hebrews. It was his persistent prayers for them that brought a downpour of rain to end a three-year drought. Charles Fillmore has explained: "This law of prosperity has been proved time and time again. All men who have prospered have used the law, for there is no other way. Perhaps they were not conscious of following definite spiritual methods, yet they have in some way set the law in operation and reaped the benefit of its unfailing action. Others have had to struggle to accomplish the same things. Remember that Elijah had to keep praying and affirming for a long time before he demonstrated the rain. He sent his servant out the first time, and there was no sign of a cloud. He prayed and sent him out again and again with the same result; but at last, after repeated efforts, the servant said he saw a little cloud. Then Elijah told them to prepare for rain, and the rain came. This shows a continuity of effort that is sometimes necessary. If your prosperity does not become manifest as soon as you pray and affirm God as your substance, your supply, and your support, refuse to give up. Show your faith by keeping up the work. You have plenty of Scripture to back you up."

A great prosperity story is contained in the old folk tale of Job, whose substance was great. According to this legend, Satan took Job's wealth, health, and family from him. Satan symbolizes man's own negative, limited concepts that are responsible for his loss of health, wealth, and happiness. It was not until Job changed his attitudes, and was again willing to "consider the wondrous works of God" in spite of his afflictions, and to pray for his friends, that he was healed. Then Jehovah gave Job twice as much as he had had before.

Prosperity Is Divinely Approved (II)

MANKIND has always desired peace and prosperity, and always will. It is a divine desire implanted in each of us. Truly a revolution is necessary, if all mankind is to realize these God-intended blessings. That revolution must come through the application of ideas that will produce peace and prosperity, rather than through strife and bloodshed.

The revolutionary ideas that can bring the world peace and prosperity can be found in the life and teachings of Jesus Christ. Emmet Fox has written: "Jesus Christ is easily the most important figure that has ever appeared in the history of mankind. It makes no difference how you may regard Him, you will have to concede that . . . the teachings attributed to Him have influenced the course of human history more than those of any other man who has ever lived; more than Alexander, or Cæsar, or Charlemagne, or Napoleon, or Washington."

We often think of Jesus as the great Healer. That He was, but He was more. Jesus understood the mental and spiritual laws of prosperity, and He used them for the universal good. As Charles Fillmore has written: "Jesus was rich toward God in that He knew how to release the creative substance implanted in Him from the beginning. This same substance is within every one of us; when released, it makes contact with the universal substance, and invisible currents of supply begin to carry their riches to us."

The Bible is still our greatest teacher of the various principles of successful living. When a sufficient number of people realize this and utilize its teachings, the Bible can again become mankind's greatest source of practical help. All of the great men of the Bible were either rich from birth, or became prosperous, or had access to riches whenever the need arose.

Jesus Christ was the master teacher of prosperity. His entire life demonstrated His interest in the subject. Even at His birth the Wise Men from the East blessed Him with gold, frankincense, and myrrh. These rich gifts symbolized the rich attitudes that we all have to give and receive.

Gold is a precious metal, symbolic of prosperity and plenty. You can give yourself a gift of gold by affirming: *"I am now blessed with plenty, plenty, plenty, in the name of Jesus Christ!"* A businessman used this statement when he was told that because he was nearing the retirement age, he would have to give up his job of long standing within a few weeks. As he continued affirming, he met a business acquaintance on the street, and while in conversation was employed by this friend to begin work on a new job.

Frankincense is a gum that is burned as an incense. It produces a pleasant aroma, a pleasant atmosphere. Whenever you do anything to produce pleasantness and beauty, either for yourself or for others, you are giving the Wise Men's gift of frankincense. If, for instance, you view some area that needs greater beauty, quietly affirm for it: *"You are now blessed with pleasantness and beauty, in the name of Jesus Christ."* The results may amaze you.

A news reporter began to study Truth; and as she trained her mind to dwell more and more upon the goodness of God and man, she began to desire beautiful surroundings. Realizing this to be her divine heritage as a child of God, she began to bless the building in which she worked. For months she daily affirmed for the walls, furnishings, and equipment in this building: *"You are now blessed with pleasantness and beauty, in the name of Jesus Christ."* One day her boss said: "For the next few days, you'll have to make your headquarters at a desk on the lower floor. This entire building is being remodeled and redecorated, and they'll begin with this floor."

Myrrh is a gum that is used to make incense, perfume, and medicine. Though myrrh is bitter, it has the power to produce sweet, harmonious, healing results. Harmonious attitudes help you to turn the bitter to the sweet. Another newspaper reporter desired to use Truth ideas in her job. Since she was a reporter on the "courthouse beat," it was her job to report the various experiences that lead people into court. It seemed a very negative assignment. A teacher suggested that she begin giving the myrrh that the Wise Men offered the Christ Child, by establishing harmonious attitudes toward her work and those about whom she wrote, thereby turning the bitter into the sweet.

It was suggested to this reporter that every time she had to write a story about a seemingly negative court case, she should realize that the people involved were subconsciously seeking spiritual blessing, and that in reality they were seeking their good and had somehow gotten off the track. She was also assured that her silent prayers and blessings for them would reach them subconsciously, and that they would be soothed and helped thereby. The prayer she used for these people was: *"You are now healed, whole, harmonious, in the name of Jesus Christ."* Whenever the events she had to write about seemed to depress or upset her, she would affirm for herself: *"I am now healed, whole, harmonious, in the name of Jesus Christ."*

She began to feel more peaceful about her work, and those about whom she wrote seemed especially blessed through their contact with her. In a number of instances, they thanked her for the positive way in which she reported their court experiences. Not long ago, another reporter declared of this woman: "For a long time I have been trying to figure out her secret. She always seems in control of herself and the situations she reports. When anyone at the courthouse has a problem, he goes to her, and she seems to have just the right thought or word of comfort and advice."

Even though Jesus has been described as being so poor that He had no place to lay His head, He had a home with His parents in Nazareth and was gladly welcomed into the homes of both rich and poor all over Palestine. Further evidence of the prosperity He enjoyed is found in descriptions of the rich apparel He wore. Jesus dressed as a rabbi, and His seamless robe was considered so desirable that the Roman soldiers cast lots for this beautiful garment at the Cross.

Even Jesus' first miracle had to do with prosperity, when He turned water into wine at a wedding feast in Cana. When the supply of wine ran out, Jesus' mother said to Him, "They have no wine." The word *mother* here symbolizes the emotional feelings of mankind. When you have a financial need, your own feelings test your reaction by reminding you of the need. But Jesus immediately took control of His feelings (as we should) by declaring: "O woman, what have you to do with me? My hour has not yet come"—in other words: "Don't expect me to rush forth to meet this need. I must first work it out within my own thinking." When Jesus had gained control of His own feelings, He said to the servants, "Fill the jars with water." They filled them to the brim. The servants symbolize our thoughts; the jars symbolize a financial need. We, too, meet our financial problems most easily when we fill our thoughts about them to the brim with ideas and affirmations and decrees of rich substance, rich supply, perfect fulfillment.

Once when I was changing jobs, and for a period would receive a lower salary, the affirmation that helped me fill my financial "water jars" to the brim was: *"I am always provided for, because I have faith in God as my omnipresent abundance."* It was amazing how I seemed to have more, even though I was receiving a lower income for a time.

During this period, I was sometimes tempted to limit myself because of the lower income. The affirmation that helped me hold to the idea of unlimited supply was: *"I have faith in God as my almighty resource and I trust God to preserve me in my prosperity."* The result was that I did not have to lower my standard of living at all. Indeed, it seemed that I *was* preserved in my prosperity, regardless of what my checkbook indicated.

At still another period when all the usual channels of supply closed to me and I was not sure where my new supply was to come from, the affirmation I used was: *"I trust the universal Spirit of prosperity in all my affairs. I trust the universal Spirit of prosperity to provide richly for me now!"* My supply began to appear from near and far, through people and channels I had never before known.

After the servants filled the water jars to the brim, Jesus instructed them, "Now draw some out, and take it to the steward of the feast"—in other words, "Be definite at this point about your desired prosperity." We often use general affirmations for prosperity, but seemingly fear to be definite. Yet, unless we do at times become very definite in our thinking about the specific prosperity we desire, we do not draw it out of the realm of universal substance in any definite form. Often our lack of demonstration is caused by our failure to be definite in our thoughts, words, decrees, and actions.

Jesus obviously had nothing against money, because He unhesitatingly called Matthew, a tax collector for the Romans, to be one of His apostles. Later He appointed Judas as treasurer for Himself and the apostles, showing His appreciation of the orderly handling of money. When a rich man came to Jesus and asked what he must do to inherit eternal life, the Scripture records that "Jesus looking upon him loved him." When Jesus told the man to sell what he had in order to inherit eternal life, it was (we believe) because He knew that the man was controlled by his possessions. Jesus' comment was, "How hard it will be for those who have riches to enter the kingdom of God!"

We gain prosperous insight by studying the

spiritual and mental laws that Jesus used to feed
the five thousand in the desert place at dusk. Of
this prosperity demonstration, Charles Fillmore
has written: "When Jesus had only a small supply He gave thanks for the little He had. This
increased that little into such an abundance that
a multitude was satisfied with food and much
was left over. Blessing has not lost its power
since the time Jesus used it. Try it and you will
prove its efficacy. The same power of multipli-
cation is in it today. Praise and thanksgiving im-
parts the quickening spiritual power that produces growth and increase in all things.

"You should never condemn anything in
your home. If you want new articles of furniture
or new clothes to take the place of those you
now have, do not talk about your present things
as old or shabby. Watch your words. See yourself clothed as befits a child of the King and see
your house furnished just as pleases your ideal.
Thus plant in the home atmosphere the seed of
richness and abundance. It will all come to you.
Use the patience, the wisdom, and the assiduity
that the farmer employs in planting and culti-
vating, and your crop will be sure."

I once knew two businesswomen who blessed
and gave thanks for the cars they were driving.
The first woman was driving a very old car. As
she praised, blessed, and gave thanks for this

car, rather than criticizing, or condemning it, her car functioned perfectly for her. As she continued to follow the example of Jesus in feeding the five thousand, by similarly praising and giving thanks for the substance at hand, it multiplied. In a short time, she was financially able to buy a new car and was given an amazingly generous trade-in allowance on the old one.

The other woman had purchased her car new and immediately began praising and blessing it. The result was that it seemed never to grow old but continued to give her unusually good service. She drove it for more than a decade before trading it in on a new one.

Charles Fillmore has explained Jesus' ability to produce apparent miracles in His use and understanding of substance: "Science tells us that there is a universal life that animates and sustains all the forms and shapes of the universe. Science has broken into the atom and revealed it to be charged with tremendous energy that may be released and be made to give the inhabitants of the earth powers beyond expression, when its law of expression is discovered. Jesus evidently knew about this hidden energy in matter and used His knowledge to perform so-called miracles."

Another prosperity principle is demonstrated in the manner in which Jesus and all His

apostles paid taxes to the Roman government.
When the question of taxes arose, Jesus did not
react negatively but told Peter to go to the sea,
cast a hook, take up the first fish that appeared,
open its mouth, and find there the money with
which to pay the taxes.

First, let us note that Jesus did not do anything to pay His taxes; He told Peter what to
do. Peter symbolizes man's mental faculty of
faith. Always our faith in the omnipresent substance is tested when we have a financial need.
As Charles Fillmore has pointed out: "What we
need to realize above all else is that God has
provided for the most minute needs of our daily
life and that if we lack anything it is because we
have not used our mind in making the right contact with the supermind." We make right contact with the supermind (God), and unlimited
substance, through faith.

Faith is an inner conviction or assurance
that there is a way to meet our financial needs.
Thus we "go . . . to the sea" by dwelling on the
sea of abundance we see all about us. The
Psalmist went to the sea of abundance when he
affirmed the words of the 23d Psalm, (which has
often been described as the "prosperity psalm").
By browsing through the Bible and dwelling on
its rich promises, by reading a book on prosperity, by reading the biography of a successful

man, or by dwelling on whatever gives you a
rich feeling of universal abundance, you "go to
the sea."

Jesus next told Peter to "cast a hook"—to
cast forth a definite idea or decree about the
need at hand. It is good to recognize mentally
that there is a need to be met and to realize that
through the universal law of supply and de-
mand, there is also a way to meet the need. You
thereby cast a definite "hook" or decree into the
sea of substance. You might do this by declaring: *"Divine Intelligence, here is the situation.
Now let there be light, guidance, understanding
about this. Let the perfect, divine idea, the perfect supply, the perfect solution, now appear."*
This opens your mind to receive the right ideas
or to make way in your affairs for the right opportunities and events that will meet the need.

Jesus next told Peter to "Take the first fish
that comes up," open its mouth, and find there
the money with which to pay the taxes. After
decreeing guidance, you should take the first idea
that comes to you, and "open its mouth"—that
is, examine the idea, dwell upon it, and let it
unfold to you the ways and means of providing
financial supply to meet your need.

I once knew a businessman who was facing
an income-tax deadline. He learned of this mental formula and decided to try it. He had had a

bad year financially and did not have the money to pay his taxes. One night when everything was quiet, he relaxed and began to think of the first step—"Go to the sea." He dwelt mentally upon the sea of substance—the omnipresent riches and supply that fill the universe. He read from Charles Fillmore's book *Prosperity;* "Even though there seems to be material lack, there is plenty of substance for all. We are standing in the very midst of it. . . . It is in the water, in the air everywhere, abounding, glorious spiritual substance. Take that thought and hold it. Refuse to be shaken from your spiritual stand in the very midst of God's prosperity and plenty, and supply will begin to come forth from the ether and plenty will become more and more manifest in your affairs." This man went to the "sea of substance" by affirming: *"I am strong, immovable Spirit substance."*

This gave him a sense of peace and an inner conviction that he would be shown how to pay his taxes. He then "cast a hook" by asking that the need be met: *"I give thanks for the immediate, complete payment of my income taxes in God's own wonderful way."* Thereafter, an idea concerning a bank loan came into his thinking. Though previously he had avoided borrowing money whenever possible, he nevertheless "opened its mouth" by meditating upon that idea and mentally exploring it from every angle. The next morning, he went to the bank, and a loan was quietly and easily negotiated. In this regard, he affirmed: *"I bless the giving and receiving of all money. I am at peace. I trust in God."* With his need met, he was able to give full attention to his business affairs, and soon had the loan paid off. Looking back on this experience, he decided to clear his mind of any negative feeling about it by declaring: *"I dissolve all financial blocks in my subconscious. Never again will I be afraid of not having money."*

Even after His resurrection, Jesus was aware of the material needs of His followers. When the fishermen had fished all night without success, He appeared and instructed them to cast their nets on "the right side" or in the right, uplifted, expectant state of mind. When they did this, their nets were laden with fish.

Paul, who has been described as the "versatile genius" of the early Christian church, had a prosperous background that prepared him for the great work that lay ahead. He and his parents were devout Jews who belonged to the well-to-do working class but who enjoyed the distinction of Roman citizenship. This was an honor that provided them with a great many privileges. Paul (at that time known as Saul)

received a fine education, studying with Gama-
liel, one of the most progressive teachers of his
time. In later life, Paul placed much emphasis
upon God as the source of man's supply, writing
to the Philippians, "My God will supply every
need of yours according to his riches in glory in
Christ Jesus." He also emphasized the necessity
for systematic giving (in order to insure systematic receiving) when he wrote to the Corinthians, "On the first day of every week, each of you
is to put something aside and store it up, as he
may prosper, so that contributions need not be
made when I come." And it was a businesswoman, Lydia of Thyatira, who first sponsored
Paul's missionary work in Europe. Her home became the meeting place of the early Christians
there.

Even the last book of the Bible, the Revelation of John, symbolically describes the new
heaven and the new earth in rich terms. The
new Jerusalem is described as a city of pure
gold, surrounded by a wall of jasper, the foun-
dations of which were adorned with precious
stones, and the gates of which were pearl.

Truly the Bible is mankind's great prosperity textbook. Begin to study it from that
standpoint and you will receive practical guidance and inspiration concerning every phase of
your life.

Prosperity from the 23d Psalm

RECENTLY a retired businesswoman said: "Forty years ago, in my study of practical Christianity, I learned that the 23d Psalm is a prosperity psalm. At the time, everything was wrong in my life. I was experiencing bad health, financial difficulties, and family problems. Upon learning of its prosperity power, I lived with the words of the 23d Psalm for months and months.

"Over and over, for all my problems, I affirmed, *'The Lord is my shepherd; I shall not want.'* Gradually my troubles were resolved. Today I am seventy-five years *young*. I am financially secure, in good health, and have no more family problems. I attribute my happy way of life to my study of practical Christianity, and especially to my constant affirmation of the 23d Psalm over the years. Yes, I'm seventy-five and I'm having a ball! Life has never been so good."

The Psalms of David are filled with prosperity affirmations. Among the chief concerns of the Psalmist were prosperity and protection for himself and his flock. In one instance, David affirmed, "Send now prosperity." At another time he decreed,

"Remember me, O Lord, when thou showest
            favor to thy people;

    help me when thou deliverest them;

that I may see the prosperity of thy chosen ones,

    that I may rejoice in the gladness of thy na-
        tion,

    that I may glory with thy heritage."

Later he sang:

        "May they prosper who love you!
        Peace be within your walls,

            And security within your towers!"

    "Praise the Lord . . .

    Wealth and riches are in his house."

Not only did David think about and decree prosperity as a shepherd boy, but he went on to experience great prosperity and success as a man. He married into wealth. Even though he

had a weak personal life, he was a great success
in his work. He unified the Hebrew tribes into
a kingdom. He helped gather materials for the
famous Temple in Jerusalem, which his son
Solomon later built. His son became one of the
wealthiest men of all times, and we have every
reason to believe that he was influenced in ac-
quiring his prosperity consciousness from David.
We can learn much about prosperity from
David, especially from his 23d Psalm, which
Charles Fillmore has described as "a treatment
to free the mind of the debt idea."

The first prosperity decree of the 23d Psalm
is:
"The Lord is my shepherd, I shall not want."

This is one of the most powerful prosperity
prayers of all! This decree is a balanced, scientific prayer, containing both affirmation *(The Lord
is my shepherd)* and denial *(I shall not want)*.
The one who makes this statement does not beg
or plead with God. He knows that he is the
beloved child of a rich Father, who wants to
supply his needs. This prayer is one of confidence and faith.

Always you will find that your needs are
met when you confidently decree that they *shall*
be met with God's help, instead of negatively
begging, pleading, hoping, fearing.

The 23d Psalm is a series of positive state-

ments. There is nothing unsure, weak, or falter-
ing in this psalm. It is a bold statement of faith
and confidence in the goodness and abundance
of God and in man's access to that goodness.

Charles Fillmore has advised: "Meet every
insidious thought, such as 'I can't,' 'I don't know
how,' 'I can't see the way,' with the declaration
'The Lord is my shepherd, I shall not want.' You
'shall not want' the wisdom, the courage to do,
or the substance to do with when you have once
fully realized the scope of the vast truth that
Almightiness is leading you into 'green pastures
. . . beside still waters.' "

He points out how you can use this first affirmation in the 23d Psalm for clearing up indebtedness:

"Do not yield to the temptation of 'easy-
payment plans.' Any payment that drains your
pay envelope before you receive it is not an easy
payment. Do not allow false pride to tempt you
to put on a thousand-dollar front on a hundred-
dollar salary. There may be times when you are
tempted to miss paying a bill in order to in-
dulge a desire for some thing. This easily leads
one into the habit of putting off paying, which
fastens the incubus of debt on people before
they realize it. It is the innocent-appearing fore-
runner of the debt habit and debt thougnt that
may rob you of peace, contentment, freedom,

integrity, and prosperity for years to come. The Divine Mind within you is much stronger than this desire mind of the body. Turn to it in a time like this, and affirm: *'The Lord is my shepherd, I shall not want' this thing until it comes to me in divine order.*

"Bless your creditors with the thought of abundance as you begin to accumulate the wherewithal to pay off your obligations. Keep the faith they had in you by including them in your prayer for increase. Begin to free yourself at once by doing all that is possible with the means you have and as you proceed in this spirit the way will open for you to do more; for through the avenues of Spirit more means will come to you and every obligation will be met."

Affirm often for your own prosperity, *"The Lord is my shepherd, I shall not want."* Decree for those who owe you and those whom you owe, *"The Lord is your shepherd, you shall not want."* As you bless others with this prosperity prayer, you open the way for their increased abundance and for your own.

If you have been doing just the opposite—begging, pleading, hoping for your prosperity rather than confidently affirming and decreeing it—you may find yourself experiencing what the Psalmist next describes:

"He makes me lie down in green pastures.

He leads me beside still waters;
 he restores my soul."

When we have not been thinking in rich, prosperous, successful terms, we often require a challenge, a problem, to bring us back to prosperous thinking. Often we are forced by our problems to "lie down in green pastures"—that is, relax and get into a prosperous state of mind again.

In the Holy Land, where everything is dry, a green pasture is a heavenly thing. It is the greatest prosperity demonstration that a shepherd can make for his flocks. He dreams of green pastures beside still waters.

Sheep are afraid of rushing waters. If they get caught in turbulent water, their wool becomes filled with water; they are weighed down, and they drown. They want and need still waters. When the shepherd cannot find still waters for his sheep, he purposely diverts some of the rushing waters into a quiet, still pool. It is the only way he can safely water his sheep.

You will often find that when your problems have not been solved, after you have applied spiritual principles to them, it is because you have gotten caught in the rush and excitement of life. You need to relax into a prosperous state of mind ("green pasture") and just be still and quiet, meditating on the riches of

God and your access to them. This leads you
"beside still waters."

This will also restore your soul by calming
your thoughts and emotions. It is only after your
soul has been restored by becoming calm, peaceful, and harmonious again that your need will
be met.

An entertainer recently heard a lecture on
the power of making prosperity decrees for
solving problems. At the time she and her husband were heavily in debt, because of operations he had undergone. They were most grateful, however, that the operations had been successful.

She was a night-club entertainer, but her income and that of her husband did not add up
to enough to pay off all the medical expenses.
They had been upset, concerned about their
debts. At the lecture she heard the speaker say,
"Get still and quiet; stop talking about your
problems and start affirming perfect, rich results." She realized that this was one method of
lying down "in green pastures, beside still
waters," so that her soul might be restored.

She and her husband agreed that they would
do this. Instead of continuing to be upset and
concerned about their debts, instead of continuing to talk about them, they would still their
fears, doubts and anxieties, and begin making

prosperity decrees. Here is what happened, according to a letter this woman wrote later:

"At the time we decided to try this method, I was employed by a night club as a professional singer and piano player, with a combo of my own. As I daily practiced decreeing prosperity affirmations, I suddenly found myself booked into one of the biggest clubs in this city of more than a million people. My salary skyrocketed overnight. Between my husband's salary and mine, we were able to pay off our many bills, as well as provide for our four small children and our home.

"As we continued to keep quiet about our previous problems and to make daily prosperity decrees, I was called upon to play at another club, owned by the same man, at more than *twice* my previous salary. It seemed unbelievable! I suddenly found myself one of the highest-paid singer-pianists in the country.

"My husband and I agreed that when our bills were out of the way I would again become a mother, wife, and homemaker, no longer working outside the home. This has now happened —in less than two years from the time we faced tremendous indebtedness. My husband was offered the best job of his life in another city. He quit his previous job of eighteen years, and we moved. As we continued affirming prosperity, new opportunities kept coming to my husband.

"We were soon transferred to still another city on his new job, where he received a promotion and raise in pay. Two months ago, we bought a home we never thought we would be able to afford. We consistently thank God for our many blessings. My husband's health has been fine, and there has been no recurrence of his illness. Furthermore, he is now in line for another promotion!"

This woman and her husband proved that it pays to "lie down in green pastures beside still waters," that this process truly "restores the soul." You can do this often. Relax into a prosperous state of mind by affirming rich ideas and rich results: *"I am rich in mind and manifestation now."* Do so quietly, in the "still waters" of your thoughts. It will restore your soul and your affairs.

Charles Fillmore speaks of this:

"We do not have to work laboriously in the outer to accomplish what the lily does so silently and beautifully. Most of us rush around trying to work out our problems for ourselves and in our own way, with one idea, one vision: the material thing we seek. We need to devote more time to silent meditation and like the lilies of the field simply be patient and grow into our demonstrations."

When you have become upset and your emotions are out of harmony, gain control of yourself and your world again by quietly decreeing: *"He restores my soul."*

"He leads me in paths of righteousness
for his name's sake."

When you are seeking guidance, when you do not know what to do, this is a good statement to use: *"He leads me in paths of righteousness for his name's sake."* The name of God is good. To decree "for his name's sake" means "for the sake of good." In other words, you are affirming, *"He guides me into right results for the sake of good."*

Every time you decree for a troublesome situation, *"Only good shall come from this"* or *"I refuse to accept anything but supreme good from this experience,"* you are saying in modern language what the Psalmist said in the words of his day.

A businessman had struggled for six months trying to rent a house he owned, without success. He then realized that he had not asked for divine guidance in the rental of this property, so he affirmed: *"I refuse to accept this situation as it appears. There is no reason for this house to remain unrented. He guideth me in paths of righteousness for His name's sake. He guideth me into right results for the sake of good in this ex-*

perience." Within a few days the house was rented.

Often our problems would be quickly solved if we would decree divine guidance and right results. Declare often: *"He guides me into right results now for the sake of good."*

"Even though I walk through the valley of the
    shadow of death,
 I fear no evil;
        for thou art with me;
    thy rod and thy staff,
        they comfort me."

The "shadow of death" here symbolizes the ending of an old experience, or perhaps the dissolution of a familiar relationship that seemed right and comfortable to us.

When situations in your life begin to change and there is nothing you can do to stop that change, do not resist or fight it. The ancients used to say: "Let go what goes. The Lord has greater and better good for you."

Let the change come! Say, *"I fear no evil, for Thou art with me."* Change is good, healthy, necessary. But it can be uncomfortable and frightening when we are going through it, unless we remember to affirm, *"I fear no evil, for Thou art with me."*

The Psalmist went further: "Thy rod and thy staff, they comfort me." The shepherd's rod was a branch cut from a bush or tree, used for chastising the sheep when they tried to stray. The rod kept them in line. The shepherd carried a staff as a symbol of rank, power, authority, strength.

The rod and staff are symbols of discipline. When you are making progress on any level of life, change comes. As it does, you must discipline yourself in order to receive the good, the blessing, from that change.

You must constantly let go of old experiences and relationships, and make way for the new and better ones. But it takes discipline of one's thoughts, emotions, and reactions in order to do so. The word *discipline* means "to train . . . to make effective," and when you undergo the discipline of change, you will always find your life improved. Eventually you will realize you have been "comforted" by the periods of discipline.

Your rod and your staff for helping you to discipline and perfect your life is, again, the idea of good. You can perfect your life and affairs by holding to this thought in the midst of changing situations: *"Only good shall come from this experience. I dare to decree, expect, and accept only supreme good from this change."* You may wish to go even further and decree: *"All change in my life has been per-*

fectly timed. All change in my life has been in accord with God's good. I have gone through all change easily to meet my supreme good."

The Psalmist then goes on to decree:

"Thou preparest a table before me in the presence of my enemies."

In Bible times, a table was considered a place of feasting, rejoicing. Often the table was laden with an abundance of rich food. The table symbolized rich, visible results.

"In the presence of my enemies" means right in the presence of changing conditions (which sometimes seem to be an "enemy," unless we have learned to pass through them nonresistantly).

The Psalmist was here decreeing that as he passed through the apparent "enemy" experiences of change and challenge, the rich, visible, happy results would manifest that would give him cause for rejoicing. Having this to look forward to made it easier for him to meet the challenges of the moment.

When you find yourself in what seems to be a time of challenge and change, in what seems to be an "enemy" situation, you can decree that happy results will be forthcoming as you affirm, *"Thou preparest a table before me in the presence of my enemies."*

It is also good to go right ahead and affirm,

along with this idea, the next decree of the Psalmist:

"Thou anointest my head with oil, my cup over-
      flows."

This is a marvelous prosperity prayer. The head symbolizes wisdom and understanding. Oil denotes wealth. The Psalmist was saying, in effect, "God has anointed my understanding with rich ideas, and with rich results. Because of this, my cup runs over. My good overflows."

Please note that the Psalmist stated this affirmation in the past tense. He was saying, in effect, "It is already done in consciousness." Our good is already finished, completed, on the invisible plane. In order to bring it forth, we have to reach that place in our thinking where we decree in faith that it is already done, manifested, even though we do not yet see visible results.

A man in the oil business learned of this prosperity prayer: *"Thou anointest my head with oil, my cup overflows."* He began to use it literally for his oil business, and found it one of the finest prosperity affirmations he had ever used. After he affirmed prosperity in the past tense, his oil business began responding to this decree with happy results.

When you truly desire an overflow of prosperity in your affairs, affirm: *"Thou hast anointed my head with oil. My cup runneth over."* Be sure to emphasize the word *hast* so that your mind will accept the thought of finished results now. This will open the way for their manifestation.

"Surely goodness and mercy shall follow me
all the days of my life;
and I shall dwell in the house of the Lord
for ever."

Regardless of what your life experiences have been up to this moment, this is a fine prayer statement to use often for gaining control of your thinking, so as to insure a good life now and in the future. Instead of dwelling upon the thought, "I've had a hard time in life," begin to think in terms of goodness in the present and future: *"Surely goodness and mercy shall follow me all the days of my life, and I shall dwell in the house of the Lord [under divine protection] for ever."*

This prayer can be the changing point for you—from defeat to victory, from lack to abundance, from weakness to health, from disappointment to happiness, from confusion to peaceful, inspired living.

An accountant had had a difficult life. As he began to reverse his thinking and dwell upon present and future blessings, everything changed for the better. As he affirmed *"Surely goodness and mercy shall follow me all the days of my life,"* he received pay raises totaling $250 a month. He was given a promotion and more responsibility in his job, and he made frequent trips for his company, both in and outside of the United States. As he continued to affirm *"Surely goodness and mercy shall follow me all the days of my life,"* he inherited a large sum of money, he and his wife built a beautiful new home, and a dream of many years came true: the way opened for them to adopt a child, though previously all channels had seemed closed to them. This man proved that regardless of past or even present failures and disappointments, great good can still come when one opens his mind to receive it. You can do so as you affirm often: *"Surely goodness and mercy shall follow me all the days of my life, and I shall dwell in the house of the Lord for ever."*

Begin now to affirm daily the prosperity decrees found in the 23d Psalm. As you do, you can gain freedom from debt, ill health, inharmony, or bondage of any kind. This inspiring psalm is filled with rich miracle prayers that can produce rich, miraculous results in your life.

Printed U.S.A.
22P-4674-20M-2-81